Miracles in Indonesia

Miracles in Indonesia

God's Power Builds His Church!

DON CRAWFORD

TYNDALE HOUSE PUBLISHERS
Wheaton, Illinois

Coverdale House Publishers Ltd.
London, England

Other books by Don Crawford:

Pueblo Intrigue
Red Star over Cuba

Library of Congress Catalog Card Number 72-75962.
ISBN 8423-4350-4
Copyright © 1972 by Tyndale House Publishers,
Wheaton, Illinois 60187.

First printing, June, 1972.

Printed in United States of America.

Contents

MALAYSIA

Atjeh Terr.
Medan

Batakland

Singapore

SUMATRA

MALAYSIA

KAPUAS RIVER

KALIMANTAN

Ketapang Terr.

Bengkulu Serawai
Tandjung Enim Terr.

JAVA SEA

Djakarta

Tora
T

Maka

Surabaja

Bandung

JAVA

Banjuwangi

Jogjakarta Batu

BALI

Denpasar

Mt. Ag

INDONESIA

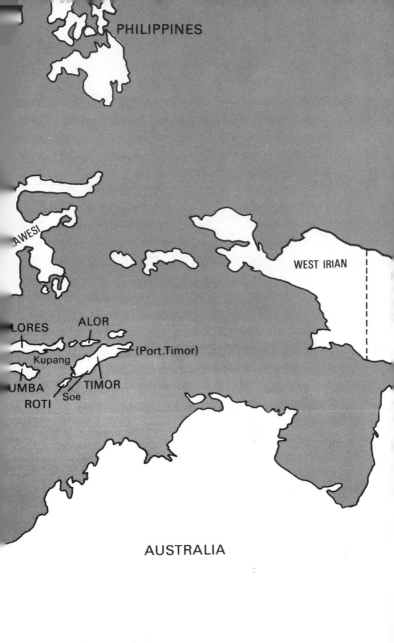

For my father,

who, like the Indonesian believers
I was privileged to observe,
has effectively translated his

Christian faith into

his daily life

"TERIMA KASIH"

(A few words of "Thanks")

I thought I detected a smile flit across the face of my host in Djakarta as he observed my bewildered countenance. I was being introduced to my living quarters in the Guest House, and some of the facilities seemed strange to me, though they were nice enough: a wide-bladed overhead fan to provide relative comfort during the tropical night; a rattan table to hold my typewriter; a large chifforobe for my clothes; and, down the hall, a well-scrubbed community bath. My problem was that for the three preceding days I had luxuriated at the sumptuous Hotel Indonesia— with its air-conditioning and pointedly Western accommodations—effectively isolated from the murky drainage ditches and pungent open sewers where Djakarta's less fortunate laundered, bathed, and eliminated. Then when I needed an extra day in Indonesia's capital city and my hotel room was unavailable, Vernon Neigenfind, director of the Inter-Mission Business Office in Djakarta, made arrangements for me to stay at the Council of Churches Guest House.

My inexperience showed when we came to the bathroom. I was studying the tiled, box-like vat of water built into one corner. It was waist high, a bit tall, it seemed to me, to climb into gracefully. But I was game.

"This is where I bathe, no doubt," I said knowingly. My subtlety failed to mask my uncertainty, however. Vernon accurately diagnosed my perplexity and, suppressing his smile, said, "Oh, you don't get into it." He picked up a plastic dipper from the ledge. "Most everyone here uses the dip method of bathing. You merely get a dipperful of water and pour it over you." He gave a dry demonstration.

I dipped out some water and poured it over my hand. The cool cascade quickly found a drain hidden ingeniously below the vat. Anticipating my next question, Vernon said, "The water here isn't usually heated."

I said nothing. I had yet to learn how refreshing a cool dip bath could be in Indonesia's humid climate.

I was also to learn appreciation for a man of such efficiency—in words as well as action—

in the position of director of IMBO, the Inter-Mission Business Office staffed by the Christian and Missionary Alliance. At the moment, however, I was struck by Vernon's statement which so accurately presaged my Indonesian trip: "I imagine there will be a lot of new experiences for you."

Indeed there were.

I am particularly indebted to Vernon Neigenfind, who added to his busy schedule the arrangement of my itinerary in Indonesia; and to the many dedicated missionaries and Indonesian Christians who gave of themselves that I could observe the extraordinary work of the Holy Spirit which is transforming that land.

I am grateful as well to John Capron, director of Home Ministries of the Worldwide Evangelization Crusade, a veteran of twelve years of missionary service in Indonesia, for insightful suggestions following his review of the manuscript. For additional valuable information about the recent history of the Indonesian church, I am most appreciative of the fine research of Frank L. Cooley, a missionary with the Board of Ecumenical Missions of the United Presbyterian Church, U.S.A. and technical adviser to the Department of Study and Research of the Indonesia Council of Churches. His presentation of facts, both in a long personal interview and in his comprehensive treatise, *Indonesia:*

Church and Society (Friendship Press, 1968), proved extensively helpful. His perceptive advice about the difficulty of obtaining meaningful statistics impressed upon me the value of concentrating on the personal aspects of the Indonesian spiritual movement. I recommend his account of the spectacular church growth in Indonesia between 1953 and 1967—from 2.5 to 4.5 million members within the churches associated with the Council alone—as an exciting presentation of ordinarily dry statistical data.

To my publisher, Kenneth N. Taylor, belongs my deep personal appreciation for his generous support of this project and his saintly patience during its lengthy preparation.

My gratitude for the assistance of these and many others could not be more sincere. And yet my deepest thanks must be reserved for another: my wife and loyal helpmeet who, during my nine-week trip abroad, was both mother and father to our five school-age children and who has shared the agony that only a writer burdened with a vital message can know.

Ultimately: "Thanks be unto God for his unspeakable gift."

DON CRAWFORD
Carol Stream, Illinois

Some readers will question the truth of certain narratives in this book—though they may not question the validity of similar miracles recorded in the Bible. What follows is, nevertheless, the result of firsthand interviews with people directly or closely involved in the phenomena occurring in Indonesia. While this account does not pretend to be a comprehensive history of this unusual movement, it does aspire to accurately detail a variety of ways in which our powerful and loving God is revealing his salvation to multitudes in that vast archipelago.

1

Timor, the Mysterious

Strange.

That one word describes many things in the Indonesian community of Soé, which rests atop one of the many mountains on the island of Timor. Its location is exotic. Its altitude is entrancing. Its people are mysterious. But in more ways than one it is a tropical paradise. One which, like many good things in life, is not arrived at without difficulties. I had my share of problems getting there, and the first thing I wanted to know when I finally reached the town on a very black night in April was when I would be able to leave again. My almond-skinned host assured me, with a complacency that emphasized the gulf between our cultures, that God would surely arrange it. Beneath his beatific smile I detected a quiet chiding for my anxiety, but from my Western point of view my worry was warranted. It had taken me almost eight bone-jolting hours to travel the seventy-five miles from coastal Kupang to mile-high Soé.

Even before the sojourn got underway I had been obliged to spend six hours in the stifling humidity of Kupang, waiting for one of the limited means of transportation up the mountain at that time of year. It was not quite the end of the rainy season, and rare trips up the miry, rutted road could be made only by truck or jeep. I made the journey in the rear of a cargo truck, along with a dozen genial Indonesians, squeezed in among the dry goods and assorted merchandise that were packed between the high sideboards up to the roof of the truck. It was 10:30 at night when we arrived in Soé—and extremely dark, for there are no street lights in the community.

My Indonesian companions, who had accepted the wait and the cramped, undulating ride with characteristic equanimity, were not concerned about a return trip, but I certainly was. The American missionary who had seen me off in Kupang had strongly urged that I check on return transportation as soon as I arrived, since trips up or down the mountain were infrequent and unscheduled. I had a reserved flight out of Kupang in a week and I didn't want to miss important appointments on other Indonesian islands. On our way up I noted that the entire journey was made without meeting another vehicle—but we passed a few that had apparently given up the struggle to conquer the trail. The casual advice of my Soé host to let God arrange the return transportation seemed absurdly mystical and highly impractical to me.

I accepted his suggestion graciously, nonetheless, and determined to make the best of the circumstances. The arduous trip had been willingly made, after all. I was in Indonesia investigating reports of an amazing church growth which had been accompanied by unusual spiritual happenings. The island of Timor, and the area surrounding Soé in particular, seemed to be the center of much of this activity. Reports had been so extraordinary—strange stories of miracles, visions, healings, even resurrections from the dead— that I was looking forward to my visit with a mixture of excitement and apprehension.

The morning after my arrival I stepped out of the small inn where I had found lodging to see such lush tropical foliage reaching across wide, verdant valleys to distant mist-blue mountains that I wondered if my long climb of the previous night had perhaps taken me to the foot of heaven itself. Abetting the illusion were the cherubic voices of children vibrantly singing hymns in a frame school building across the street. Other qualities about Soé contributed to its ethereal atmosphere.

While the singular beauty of the surrounding jungle was esthetically breathtaking, the altitude was literally so. It offered blessed, cool relief from the oppressive coastal humidity, but it gave me a heady feeling. The vegetation advanced its own aura of unreality: it just didn't seem possible for trees to grow that tall. Exotic tropical varieties challenged familiar pines and locusts, the latter with two-foot-long pods, to stretch dizzyingly into the sky. It was unlike anything I had previously observed in my earthly experience.

It was in the people, however, that I felt closest to a heavenly realm. I first encountered this other-worldly characteristic the night of my arrival. My visit had been unannounced since telephone service does not connect Soé and Kupang. The truck driver secured me a guide, a short, thin man perhaps sixty years old who seemed to be the only person still up in the darkened town. The driver asked him to take me to the principal of the local Bible school, who I had been assured would act as my host. The small man insisted on carrying my luggage. Remembering the fees sometimes charged Westerners at oriental airports, I wondered how many

Principal Sardjito Martosudarmo stands in front of the Soé Bible School. Lumber for the building and classroom furniture was ported from nearby forests by the students.

rupiahs he might expect for lugging the case, heavy with recording and photographic equipment, from the truck to the principal's quarters and then to the inn. But when I asked the charge, he shook his head almost reproachfully and spoke rapidly in Timorese. My host explained, "He is glad to do it for you, as a fellow Christian." I gave him my embarrassed thanks.

My Soé host was a youthful, smiling Javanese with a typically unpronounceable name —Sardjito Martosudarmo. I was able to master only the first name and gladly followed his advice simply to call him Sardjito (Sar-GEE-toe). Although he had just been awakened, he greeted me warmly upon our encounter. His first words after our introduction were, "Let us pray together." He offered his prayer in his native tongue, which I could not understand, but I could not mistake the artless sincerity with which he spoke. As I spent the following days with him—he not only arranged many interviews but also acted as my interpreter—I could tell that his prayerful attitude was not feigned. Nor was it unusual among the believers I met during my Soé stay.

The first time we went to visit a pastor of a large church in Soé, Reverend Daniel (many Indonesians use but one name), Mrs. Daniel informed us that he was praying. We waited for some time and at length made an appointment to return in the evening after rest time. As in most tropical areas, Indonesians, who arise before dawn to begin their day's work, take a rest during the heat of the afternoon.

I arrived early at Sardjito's room that evening for our walk to Pastor Daniel's. There was no reply to my knock, and, wondering if he might still be resting, I peered through the open door to catch Sardjito at his desk in prayer. An open Bible rested on the desk top.

At the Daniels' I was again greeted affably, and with prayer. Anxious to launch into my investigation, I immediately set up my tape recorder. This act seemed to disturb the minister. In English I asked Sardjito what was wrong. He explained that the pastor, like himself and fellow believers, was extremely cautious about being quoted. They relied completely on God for livelihood and did not want his unusual blessings to be exploited for their personal glory.

"What kind of blessings?" I wanted to know, assuring them that my intentions were to give credit where credit was due. Hesitantly, Mr. Daniel began to unravel a sometimes bizarre history of the Christian Church in Soé.

Missionaries from Holland brought Christianity to the area when the Dutch ruled Indonesia as the Netherlands East Indies. While the novelty of the new religion attracted many, it did not break the strong hold of witchcraft on the people. Even among church members, the fear of evil spirits persisted to the extent that many—including some pastors—preferred to use their fetishes to placate the spirits rather than trust God to conquer them.

It was in such a state of nominal Christianity and practical animism that an evangelistic team from the island of Java found the Soé congregation in the summer of 1965. The evangelists were largely Indonesians, students from a Bible school in Batu, East Java, accompanied by a German Lutheran instructor in the school. The Indonesian-to-Indonesian ministry, aimed at fostering a complete trust in God, proved effective. As brave church leaders broke with their occult practices and escaped harm by the evil spirits, others followed their example. Amulets, which represented vital power over the imperious spirits, were burned to prove the seriousness of the new commitment.

Pastors who were initially suspicious became convinced by these and other results that something indeed had grabbed hold of their people. Prayer meetings were set up and eagerly attended. Contributions showed a marked increase. The heavy drinking of palm wine ceased. The chewing of the betel nut for its narcotic-like effect was curtailed. Youth, traditionally the hardest to reach spiritually, were the most responsive. They formed evangelistic teams of their own to take this new-found gospel of deliverance to outlying villages.

Calls to enter an evangelistic ministry came to young people in unusual fashion. Nahor Leo, a high school athlete with a reputation as a rebel, was stirred by a dynamic challenge to Christian service given by the headmistress of a Soé school. Later, studying in his room in Pastor Daniel's home with two fellow students, he suddenly called out, "Who turned out the light?" Assured it was still burning, Leo stumbled to his bed. "I'm going to rest."

He slept a few minutes. Then, as if wrenched from the bed, he fell to the floor and appeared to be struggling with an invisible force. Leo groped his way to his clothes box and thrust his hand to its bottom, then pulled up the root of a plant which was wound with red string. "Yes," Leo muttered, as if answering the unseen visitor, "this is my *djimat.*"

Leo's companions recognized the strange object as an instrument of witchcraft. "It's true," Leo spoke again. "I have used it to ask the spirits to help me win races and to attract girls." The unusual conversation continued for a moment. Then Leo collapsed on the floor.

"What's the matter? Who were you talking to?" one of the boys shouted. Leo slowly turned his sightless eyes toward his companions. At length the white-faced youth replied, "I saw the Lord. He made me reveal the *djimat* I had never given up. He told me he wanted me to serve him alone. And . . ." his voice trembled . . . "he told me I must have Pastor Daniel pray for me—or I will die. Would you get him, please?"

Pastor Daniel came swiftly at the desperate summons. After a prayer of confession, the fetish was burned. Then, reminiscent of the Apostle Paul when he was ministered to by the man of God, Leo's sight was restored.

Evangelistic team leaders meeting for a prayer-and-fellowship session in Soé get their picture taken by a visiting American missionary. Pastor Daniel stands third from right. (Photo by David Mitchell)

And, like Paul, Leo became a persuasive evangelist, inspiring others to follow the Christian way.

It was the zeal of young leaders like Nahor Leo who formed wide-roving evangelistic teams that fanned the religious fire in Timor, Mr. Daniel told me, and continuing "signs and wonders" have fueled the flame. For in every case of a supernatural occurrence, there has followed a significant turning to the Christian faith. Sardjito showed me two thick volumes in which he had recorded many of these phenomena. Even in black and white, some of the events proved hard to accept. For example: among the dated entries, which included accounts of miracles, descriptions of visions, and numerous prophecies of Christ's impending return, were several verses of songs that had been taught to young Timorese believers by unusual means.

In one case, village children on their way home from school heard singing coming from a rock. They stopped to listen and learned a song about Jesus' return, which they sang as they continued on their way. In another situation, the howling wind brought words of comfort to a youthful evangelist caught in a tropical storm. Another time, a dove taught village youngsters, whose parents had refused to believe in Christ, a song of assurance. I tried to hide my skepticism as Sardjito interpreted the songs for me. Later, at a songfest, Sardjito's Bible school students sang for me the very songs that reputedly had been taught by the stone, the wind, and the bird.

I had already heard about some of the early Soé miracles from my missionary friend in Kupang, Marion Allen of the Christian and Missionary Alliance. In visits to Soé during dry seasons he was able to investigate the happenings there. He had told me that almost every type of New Testament miracle had been repeated in the Soé area. One evangelistic team, for example, had gotten to their destination by walking across a flooded mountain stream. At first they had dismissed the feeling that they should walk on the water even though it had come to the team leader after prayer about the problem. After three successive prayer sessions, with the same apparent answer, the leader took a tentative barefoot step into the water. When he did not sink, the others followed—to the amazement of stranded travelers who witnessed the strange event from both sides of the stream.

Another team, desiring to celebrate the Lord's Supper but having no wine, were in a similar fashion instructed to use water from a nearby spring. As at the wedding Christ attended in Cana, the water, when drunk for the communion celebration, had become wine. On a hike around the Soé area, Sardjito showed me the spring from which the water-turned-to-wine had come.

Mr. Allen had talked to both of the major participants in another drama. An elderly woman among the mourners at the funeral of a young boy felt a strong impression to pray for the lad's life. At first she resisted the impulse. The boy had been dead several hours and in that climate it was imperative that an unembalmed body be buried soon after death. But her feeling persisted. When it came time to put the lid of the wooden coffin in place, she felt compelled to act. She asked if she could offer a prayer. The ceremony was

With Timor's rugged mountain panorama in the background, Sardjito (left) takes a stroll in Soé with Rev. and Mrs. Manuain.

stopped to humor the old woman. While she was praying, the boy stirred, then rose up.

To many observers the fact that the "dead" boy is alive today represents a miracle. But to the believers in Soé the miracle lies rather in how the event was useful in bringing a large number of animist worshipers to faith in Christ. Sardjito and the Soé church's two pastors, Rev. Daniel and Rev. Binjamin Manuain, all asserted that such occurrences—as well as the testimony of those who had been delivered from the grip of witchcraft—spurred a remarkable growth of Christianity on the island. From Indonesian statistical sources I learned that in the first three years of the movement the Christian population of Timor grew by 200,000.

It was a timely revival. For, in addition to the animism which held people in the bondage of fear, a subtler destroyer was invading the land. Communism, with its materialistic promises and the support of Indonesia's President Sukarno, was capturing the imagination of many church members. Communistic ideals, of course, were not compatible with the renewed faith. At the height of the strife an attempt was made to kill Pastor Daniel. The grass roof of his house was set afire one night as he and his family slept. With the dry roof like tinder, the arson would have quickly accomplished its goal had not an unseasonal rain—"sent by God," Mr. Daniel pointed out—quenched the flames. Communism itself was snuffed out of the republic in a political upheaval shortly thereafter.

As the recitation of the strange events fell on my Western ears, I wondered if I had come across an extremely imaginative group of people. Yet I was captivated by the Soé Christians' ingenuous sincerity and absolute trust in God. The mystical atmosphere apparently affected my own feelings, for I was no longer bothered about when—or whether— I would be able to return to Kupang and the rest of my itinerary. I had prayed for transportation down; if God wanted me to make my appointed flight, he would arrange it.

On Sunday morning I attended a worship service with my Timorese friends. Since I was aware that Soé's simple carpentry and furniture-making was all done locally, using trees felled in the nearby forests, I was surprised to see an imposing, raised pulpit above the altar, from which the robed pastor delivered his sermon. Pastor Manuain's message, as interpreted for me by Sardjito, was biblically oriented and spiritually profound. But I was more impressed with the congregation. Worshipers filled every available seat in the large building although this was the second sermon, delivered in Indonesian rather than in their native Timorese. And their hymn singing, done without accompaniment, was so unrestrained yet so harmonious—so alive— that it spoke volumes about the meaningfulness of their faith.

Resting in my room that afternoon, I tried to reconstruct the past several days. I'd have many experiences to look back on if I ever got out of Soé. As the memories mingled, I dozed. Then the urgent squeal of brakes outside my window jolted me awake. I got up to investigate. Motor transportation had been so rare that I was surprised to see a jeep stop at the inn. I wondered, rather whimsically, if this might be the transportation that was to be provided for my trip to Kupang. I would need it on that day if I were to make my scheduled flight. I wasn't overly optimistic, however, for the jeep looked just like the one I had seen sitting outside Soé's "city hall."

I stepped into the lobby just as three men entered through the outside door. One of them was a Westerner. I introduced myself, hoping he could speak English. He could. He was an American emigrant to Australia, he said, a rancher who had been sent to this remote area by a large cattle company to find grazing land. He had stopped here with his Indonesian helpers to eat supper before going on down the mountain.

They were headed for Kupang!

As calmly as I could I explained that I was seeking transportation there myself.

The rancher smiled perceptively. "In Indonesia one always makes room," he said.

I nodded, recalling the crowded ride up the mountain. We talked a few minutes, making arrangements to leave for Kupang right after the evening meal, then I rushed to tell Sardjito.

It was a bittersweet moment. While I was excited at this obvious answer to prayer, I was saddened at the realization that I must soon leave my Shangri-La. An inscrutable smile made Sardjito's face radiant as I delivered the news. "Isn't God wonderful," he said. It was more a statement than a question, and I felt ashamed at my own doubt. That my transportation had been provided at just the right moment didn't surprise him at all. Of course, we prayed together, thanking God for his faithfulness, and I was soon on my way down the mountain, just as Sardjito had predicted.

Once back to the realities of "civilization"—including the lowland's oppressive humidity—I began to wonder about all I had seen and heard. Had my perception been clouded by Soé's exotic location? Was what I had been told a product of the tellers' imagination? Or of mine? I could hardly refute my own experience in getting down the mountain, though I knew the arrival of the Australian rancher could easily be explained away as mere coincidence. Impulsively, I inserted a tape into my recorder and listened to the Soé students' fervent a cappella singing. Once again I heard the songs that they believed had been taught by a stone and a bird and the wind. I didn't doubt God's ability to do great and wonderful acts, but I'd never known him to do things quite that way.

I was not alone in my skepticism. Even before my trip to Soé I had encountered it among Christians in Indonesia. Mere mention of the Timorese revival was enough to open a debate about its reliability. I was to learn, however, that the closer I came to Soé the more the unusual events were accepted as the work of God's Spirit. About one thing most of the Christians I met in Indonesia agreed: that God was indeed working in a mysterious way throughout the islands. But his work could not be characterized. What was done in Timor was not echoed in Sumatra, for example, where multitudes likewise had turned to Christianity. In fact, if anything could typify the work of the Holy Spirit in Indonesia it would have to be diversity.

Strange, indeed.

2

The Land God Claimed

My first glimpse of Indonesia was the lush green foliage and the ubiquitous red-tiled roofs of Western Java as they appeared beneath the jet bringing me to Djakarta, the nation's capital. We landed just as the sun was going down, and I could observe how quickly and deeply darkness descends at this proximity to the equator. It was dusk as I left the plane, but by the time I had crossed the long concrete walkway and entered the terminal night had fallen. I was making my way through customs when Missionary Vernon Neigenfind spotted me and welcomed me to Djakarta.

As we drove to the Hotel Indonesia in Vernon's Chevrolet, I got a closer look at Djakarta's broad, six-lane highways and its many high-pillared statues which had been visible from the air. They are legacies, I learned, of the extravagant Sukarno era which nearly bankrupted the nation. Before long we reached the hotel where we discussed my immediate travel plans. It was Saturday night. Vernon would pick me up for a church service Sunday morning, to be followed by a tour of Djakarta. On Monday I would start my interviewing with church leaders and laymen which he had scheduled.

The Sunday afternoon tour of Djakarta presented me with a view of Indonesia's kaleidoscopic diversity, so conspicuous in the capital city. Magnificent government embassies and large shopping marts intermingle with piled-together huts and crowded, open markets. Limousines and oxcarts simultaneously travel the city's modern thoroughfares. On the outside "slow" lanes of the highways, myriads of *betjak* drivers seek customers for their rear-propelled pedicabs among a multitude of pedestrians. I could easily believe I was on one of the world's most densely populated islands and in Indonesia's largest city, which has a population of nearly five million, many of whom seemed to be right there along the road.

It started to rain as we turned off the expressway at the outskirts of the city onto a barely-two-lane macadam road. The houses along it, while still clustered closely togeth-

A bevy of betjak *drivers pedal their pedicab passengers along a crowded city street on populous Java.*

er, were more pretentious than the shacks we had seen along the superhighway. Terra cotta roofs were shedding their rain water onto small boys splashing under the drain spouts. I had been warned about the unpredictability of Indonesia's April weather, but I wasn't prepared for the continued mugginess that was unrelieved by the rain. Despite the steady downpour, a soccer game was in progress in an open area along our way. The barefoot players were a flurry of brown skins and bright-colored shorts splashing after a slippery ball. As yet unadjusted to the climate, I was amazed that anyone could possess the energy to play so enthusiastically in the steamy heat.

A few kilometers into the green countryside away from Djakarta, Vernon stopped the car and we got out. The rain had subsided, and we walked in a misty drizzle toward a simple structure beside a farmhouse. It looked like nothing more than four corner posts supporting a roof. "It's a hallowed site despite the austerity of its architecture," Vernon told me. "We'll have to take off our shoes."

We mounted a few steps to a platform that surrounds the object of veneration: a two-foot-wide well. It became the temporary burial plot for six army generals killed by Communist insurgents in 1965. While the shrine commemorates a political convulsion, it is important symbolically to Christians, also, for the country's surging spiritual revival is linked to this political upheaval.

Communism was introduced to these islands as early as 1901 when Marxist organizers infiltrated newly formed trade unions. But not until the nation gained its independence in 1949 did Soviet ideology claim a significant following. By 1965 Indonesian Communists boasted the largest party membership outside Russia and Red China. They also enjoyed the favor of Indonesia's flamboyant President Sukarno, who had been named to his position "for life" in 1963.

Heady with power, Communist leaders planned their grab for complete control on October 1, 1965. Their first objective was to eliminate military resistance by liquidating eight Indonesian Army generals. In the early hours of October 1 six of the generals were captured and killed by Communist guerrillas. Their bodies were mutilated by the *Gerwani,* Communist women's organization, and stuffed into the well outside Djakarta.

Two generals, Suharto and Nasution, narrowly escaped execution and led the armed forces in a successful counterattack. General Suharto, who became acting president, steered the nation through the rocky months following the coup attempt. With support of a coalition of "action fronts," he accomplished the legal outlawing of the Communist Party. He also kept the popular Sukarno in the political background without power until Sukarno's death in 1971. And he pulled inflation-ridden Indonesia back from an economic collapse produced by his predecessor's prodigality. Unfortunately, the government's victory opened the way to a savage anti-Communist butchery among civilians, resulting in an estimated 400,000 deaths before it was brought under control.

Some observers claim this violence accounts for the dramatic religious upsurge in Indonesia, for the extreme danger of being labeled Communist in the post-coup period prompted thousands to become officially "Christian" or "Muslim,"—anything which would in effect say, "See, I'm not a Communist, for I believe in God." The fear of severe anti-Communist reprisal plus an executive order requiring every citizen to associate with a religious group unquestionably affected the religious picture in Indonesia. One missionary told me that at his station in Madiun, East Java, multitudes joined religious institutions in an impulse movement that had very little spiritual significance. "The Catholic church in our town increased by 5,000 members in the year following the coup attempt," he said. "Mosques that were just about deserted became so brimmed over that they were building onto all of them."

This external motivation can explain only part of the rapid multiplication of church membership during this period, however. It is known, for example, that many nominal Muslims turned to the Christian way not out of fear but out of revulsion toward their fellow Muslims' slaughter of suspected Communists. And much of the revival—which persists today, half a decade beyond the abortive coup—is completely separate from the political unrest, although it is oriented to it in time.

But one important aspect of the attempted coup makes the Communist rebellion significant to the Christian movement and national life of Indonesia: After the Communists were routed, lists were discovered of people they had planned to eliminate or expel. In addition to political opponents, the lists included Indonesian religious leaders and all foreign missionaries. Had the coup been successful, the work of the Church would have suffered drastically throughout the country.

A few days after my visit to the memorial well, I talked with a former member of parliament who, like many Christians I met in Djakarta, considers the Communist defeat a miracle of God. "The Communists were, after all, just two heartbeats away from victory," Darius Marpaung told me in an eloquent reference to the surviving generals. Marpaung, who heads the Indonesian Christian Workers Union, was a leader of popular forces that helped strip Communists of their power. He gave me a behind-the-scenes look at the precarious days following the coup attempt.

His union, he admitted, was not an influential one. It came into prominence only after the attempted coup. Ten years before, when Marpaung had launched the ICWU, he couldn't even gain support for it from the Christian churches. There were many Christian workers, to be sure, but since the majority of laborers were Communists, churchmen feared the ICWU was another leftist plot to infiltrate the church. Although it had gained the confidence of Christian laborers by 1965, the ICWU was still a fledgling union when, in the struggle for power following the murder of the generals, it joined other non-Communist labor groups to form the All-Indonesian Labor Action Front. Perhaps because of Marpaung's spirited patriotism—he had been imprisoned three times during Indonesia's campaign for independence from the Netherlands—the ICWU representative was elected head of this united group. And when the laborers joined other "action fronts," including the passionate student corps, Marpaung was asked to head the whole movement.

Marpaung was surprised—and scared. His fear was not due to the personal danger, although several activists had already died, but because of the singular importance of the position at that time in Indonesian history. He was looked upon to lead extra-government forces in the desperate struggle to preserve the country from Communism. The weight of such a burden drove him to his

Darius Marpaung (left), head of the Indonesian Christian Workers Union, chats with Ais Pormes, Indonesian Campus Crusade director and ICWU chaplain.

close friend, ICWU Chaplain Ais Pormes. "What should I do?" he asked. "Why was I chosen for such a task?"

Pormes reached for his Bible. "It may be that God had selected you for this hour," he said gravely. He opened the Book and handed it to Darius. "Read Romans 8:31."

Marpaung studied the text: "If God be for us, who can be against us?"

"Let's pray," Pormes suggested.

When they raised their heads, Darius said quietly, "I'll do it."

The next day Marpaung met with all the

representatives of the action fronts. He called the meeting to order and boldly stated, "Gentlemen, let's pray." There was no gainsaying the crucialness of the hour. The leaders readily agreed to call upon God for help.

For the next six months Marpaung and other leaders addressed demonstrations, exposed the faults of the Communists, urged the people to accept a temporary military government, and conducted operations to frustrate Sukarno's leftist-inclined cabinet—such as blocking the doors to government offices and suspending government business for three days. On the eleventh day of March, 1966, Sukarno bowed to pressures of the military command and an aroused citizenry and authorized General Suharto to take all necessary steps for safeguarding the nation and the president.

Suharto's first action was to outlaw the Communist Party. His next step was the purging of Communists from Sukarno's cabinet. Here he had to walk carefully, for Sukarno still commanded a great deal of respect from the people. Public support would have to be generated by the allied action fronts. Darius Marpaung's neophyte popularity would be pitted against the people's twenty-year devotion to their nation's founder.

Using radio, television, newspapers, and public-address vans, the action fronts called for a mass rally opposing the cabinet. On the day of the rally Marpaung walked to the government square where the people had congregated. He was overwhelmed by the sea of people. Newspapers estimated the crowd at three million, which Darius doubted because that would have been three-fourths of Djakarta's total population. Nevertheless, the support was dramatic. Before stepping forward, Marpaung bowed his head in prayer. "Lord," he whispered, "I can't do it alone." Then he walked to the podium and, forgetting the ten microphones there, tried to reach the vast audience with his shouting.

It was almost as if someone else were delivering the fervid speech, Marpaung told me. His larynx was so overworked that he could only whisper afterward. But his appeal was successful. The massing of support for democratic policies by the coalition of intellectuals, students, and laborers convincingly demonstrated to Sukarno that his popularity was limited. A new cabinet would be formed with Communists and their fellow travelers removed.

Darius Marpaung's name was presented for the post of Minister of Labor on the reformed cabinet. Understandably, Sukarno opposed Marpaung's candidacy. Although his power had been broken, Sukarno still wielded influence, and General Suharto was pursuing a deliberately slow pace in assuming government reins. On March 27 a new cabinet—a compromise group which Suharto said represented only "the maximum possible progress in the first stage"—was announced. Marpaung's name was not on the list.

Although Darius was to serve his country later as a member of parliament, he now felt rebuffed and rejected. He went home that evening to slip into merciful sleep. At one o'clock the following morning, however, he was aroused by an insistent knock. He went to the door and was met by a bayoneted rifle. It was held by a man in uniform, buttressed by a platoon of soldiers. The man ordered Marpaung to dress and accompany him. Darius returned to his bedroom, the platoon leader following to watch at the door.

"Who is it?" Darius' wife wanted to know.

"Communists, I think," he answered quietly. "They are in military dress, but I don't know who else would want to get rid of me. Let's pray together, for I may never see you again." As the guard looked on, the couple placed each other in God's keeping.

Tropical nights are characteristically dark, but this was a particularly black night for Darius Marpaung. At an army detention barracks where he was taken, he learned that he was now a military prisoner. Darius was bewildered. Was the fear of personal attack that he had lived with for months at last being consummated—but by his army allies instead of Communist enemies?

As one day tediously followed another and no action was taken—no explanation given for the confinement—Darius had to renew his trust in the Christ he had accepted years before in his native Batakland, North Sumatra. He passed the time singing Batak hymns, not knowing what was happening outside.

When word got around that Darius Marpaung was a political prisoner, his followers responded with mass demonstrations. Students threatened to picket the army barracks day and night until Marpaung was set free. A mourning procession, with Marpaung's picture carried in oriental funeral style, was conducted in Bandung. Prayers were offered throughout the country in his behalf.

Four days after his arrest, Darius was released. A major general apologized to him for the action, explaining at last the detention's purpose: to prevent Marpaung from organizing a demonstration against the new cabinet which had not included him. The prisoner's genuine shock at the charge convinced the officer that Marpaung was sincere in his denial of any retaliation. The rueful general even offered to make a public statement of apology for Marpaung's imprisonment, but Darius declined the embarrassing action.

Overcoming any disappointment or bitterness he might have felt about the unfortunate circumstances was his deep gratitude at being able to help preserve his country's freedom, particularly her religious freedom. Now the work of the Church could go on in Indonesia—a work of God that Marpaung would never have dared to hope for in his beloved land.

3

Survivors of Slaughter

While I was still in Djakarta, I learned about Indonesia's reverence for basic freedoms. These freedoms are embodied in the country's historic *Pantja Sila* (Sanskrit for "Five Principles"). The very first element is affirmation of a belief in God. The others—belief in nationalism, humanity, democracy, and social justice—arise from this primary religious principle. But I also learned that the ravage and terror done "in the name of God" to protect these concepts after the attempted Communist coup were hardly in keeping with any of them.

Hundreds of thousands of Communists and suspected Communists were seized and many executed without trial by military troops and fanatic religious groups. In Bali whole villages that had embraced Communism were destroyed—the men killed, the women and children run off, the buildings burned. Religious leaders on that predominantly Hindu island justified the murderous frenzy as a purging of the land from evil. The Communists there blundered badly in deriding and attempting to undermine the island's cultural and religious tradition which are inextricably intertwined.

On other islands, too, "holy wars" were waged against known and suspected Communists. In parts of Sumatra, killings by incensed Muslims took a heavy toll. Throughout the outer islands there were purges of Communists. On North Sulawesi Communists were executed—not by Muslims or Hindus—but by impassioned Christians.

The killing of Communists was greatest on the largely Muslim island of Java, where the Communist Party was strongest. Here the Communists had paid lip service to the *Pantja Sila* in a compromise that attracted many to their party. The densely-populated island, though extremely fertile, has too many people for its tillable acreage; it was an easy convert to the socialistic promise of land reform. But the Communists' fatal error was in taking over Muslim land and quashing the *Ansor* youth of the Islamic Teachers' Party. In places like Kediri, East Java, Muslim youth groups seeking Communist victims had the blessing of the local Muslim leader, who called the massacre the "will of God." So many people were killed on Java that the disposal of bodies became a serious problem.

Not every non-Communist was happy about the slaughter. A professor at Gadjah Mada University in Jogjakarta expressed the discontent: "The anti-Communists certainly had a grudge, but there was no need to kill children, too. In one family, women, children over six, everybody was killed. They called themselves religious people, but they killed like pigs." Many educators and students, like those at Gadjah Mada, were disturbed by the pogrom. They felt poignantly its toll, for youth were extensively involved in the bloodbath, either as executioners . . . or as victims. As at other schools, many gaps appeared among the ranks of Gadjah Mada's 24,000 students.

Gadjah Mada and a number of other colleges and universities in and around Jogjakarta make it the educational and cultural center of Indonesia. Here the ancient arts of batik dyeing and silver smithery have been preserved along with centuries-old Buddhist and Hindu shrines. Thanks to missionary John Smith, I talked with a number of students who visit student centers established in Jogjakarta by Southern Baptists. In my interviews I learned how the grisly aftermath of the Communists' attempted coup contributed to the growth of the Javanese Christian church.

Not surprisingly in this Islamic stronghold, all the students I talked to were Muslim or formerly Muslim. They told similar stories—some of gnawing skepticism about the faith into which they had been born, most of concern about their government's political turn toward the left, all of shock at the brutal murder of the generals, and many of revulsion at the religiously oriented purge of the Communists. Typical of my interviewees was a sensitive student named Beni, who was completing his requirements for a medical degree.

Beni was born in Surabaja in 1941 to a well-to-do Muslim family. His parents were able to provide him with superior private schooling, and in 1960 they sent him to the university at Jogjakarta. He was at the midpoint of his schooling when this area became the scene of one of history's worst orgies of violence in the last few months of 1965. Because families of Communists met the fate of party members, students were not immune from the savagery; often it was student against student.

Like many other Muslim students, Beni was recruited to seek revenge for the Communist excesses that climaxed in the murder of the six generals. As a medical student dedicated to the preservation of life, Beni could not condone the killings. He was amazed at the zeal with which some of his fellow students accepted weapons and the challenge for revenge given by the army. Like plotters in a lurid novel, young captains laid plans to ferret out and destroy every Communist in the area. When they called for unanimous accord among the assembled students, Beni demurred. "I just can't do it," he said.

"Why not?" one of the leaders growled.

"I'm a medical student," Beni started to explain.

"Good! We'll need you in case we are wounded," someone exclaimed.

The suggestion provided an expedient compromise. Beni agreed to become an auxiliary to the plot, but he could never master his revulsion toward it. To take a fellow human's life without due process of law was unthinkable to him, yet he witnessed nightly the roundup and gruesome execution of suspected Communists. The chanted prayers which preceded every foray seemed demonic incantations designed to whet the fury of the hunters. Once captured by the fanatic student band, suspects had little hope of proving their innocence or their allegience to Allah before feeling the terrible wavy-bladed *kris*. What kind of a God, Beni wondered, would permit such bloodshed in his name?

The mad ritual of cleansing lasted but a few weeks, yet Beni will never forget the experience. While the loathsome nighttime slayings seemed monstrous to him, the daytime conciliation of the Christians was even more baffling. Representing only a fraction of the island's population, Java's Christians faced as great a threat from the Communists as anyone—but their attitude was strangely charitable. Instead of cooperating in the destruction of their enemy, the Christians preferred to help the needy. They buried abandoned bodies; they sheltered widows and the orphans produced by the purge; and, if Muslim suspicions were correct, they even protected Communists' lives.

Beni was not alone in his awe at the Christians' behavior, though he wasn't ready to go as far as many nominal Muslims who renounced their own faith to join with the Christians. He took his confusion with him to the university lecture halls. There he could see the empty seats where classmates, members of Communist families, had once sat; and, in his memory he could still see the faces of those who had met the ritualistic death of the *kris*.

Beni desperately sought ways to push the unwelcome recollection from his mind. When he heard about the English-language courses being offered at the Baptist student centers, he decided to enroll. The center Beni entered for his first class looked much like the reference room of a college library, with students studying quietly at tables, surrounded by the periodicals and resource volumes that lined the wall. The cordial American instructor introduced herself as Mrs. John Smith.

John and Nelly Smith had arrived in Indonesia seventeen months ahead of the political upheaval. After a year's language study—fortunately, the Indonesian language forged by Sukarno's linguists is a simple one—the Smiths were ready for assignment. When they were asked to work among the 45,000 students in Jogjakarta, they were initially reluctant; for neither had been trained for student work. But after extensive prayer they felt satisfied that this was where they should start their Indonesian ministry. They became directors of the first Southern Baptist student center in Jogjakarta just days before the Communists attempted to take over the government. The new missionaries, like many Christian workers in Java, found themselves in a unique position to witness to the love of God while much of the island was experiencing the hatred of man.

The Smiths saw their work flourish as they encountered hundreds of students, many of them tormented Muslim youth, who took advantage of a quiet, lighted place to study away from crowded bamboo dwellings or claimed the opportunity to learn English from one who knew the language intimately. One by one the students would seek the

Smiths out to learn more about the Christianity that the Americans could only hint at in their academic contacts. From the student centers grew a church group and a gospel outreach to thousands of bewildered Communists—those imprisoned in military arrests before the murderous purge—and to villagers who were likewise in spiritual turmoil.

Beni was one of the scores of frustrated Jogjakarta students who responded to the sympathetic concern of people like the Smiths. He sensed that these Christians, like some of his countrymen who had befriended the victims of the Communist purge, possessed a quality of self-giving love that other religious followers did not have. He had to find out what it was. On a pretext of seeking more information about an assignment, Beni visited Mr. and Mrs. Smith at the student center one evening. After the assignment had been clarified, Beni cautiously approached the real subject on his mind. "You're Christians, aren't you?" The Smiths agreed. "Well, could you tell me about Christianity?"

"What would you like to know?" John asked. He had heard this request often enough to know it was best to let the seeker express his personal need.

"I saw so much killing in the name of God— I even helped, though I did not kill anyone myself. . . ." Beni groped for words to express the tumult in his mind. "But while we

Jogjakarta "taxi"

were killing I saw Christians show so much
love—and also in the name of God . . . I want
to know more about this religion."

Carefully the Smiths explained the revelation of God through his Son, Jesus Christ,
who commands love instead of hate. At first,
the Americans' explanation seemed too sim-

ple for Beni. It was incredible that by merely accepting Jesus as the Son of God a person could experience God's love. Not that he could argue with the results of such belief—that had been convincingly demonstrated to him!

Beni's questions were numerous and deadly earnest. The Smiths' answers were reasoned and equally sincere. Jesus Christ, the same prophet mentioned in the Koran, but more than that—the equal of God—had died for every sin, even those as gross as Beni had been a partner to and was even now giving assurance through his Spirit that his followers could live forever in his love.

"But how can this be?" Beni countered.

"You just have to trust him, Beni."

Ultimately, there was no room left for argument. Beni had to either accept Christ's claims or reject them. It was with genuine relief that he made his decision.

All that Beni had seen in the macabre ritual of death and in the contrasting compassion of Christianity had prepared him for the moment, when he, along with thousands of other grieving Javanese, traded the vengeful law of religion for the regenerating love of Jesus Christ.

4

Spirit-Taught Christians

God was working in Indonesian hearts long before the religious-political upheaval—but hardly by Western-style promotional schemes. "This is about as far away from Madison Avenue as you can get," an American in East Java told me. His reference was not only to the isolation of the area from modern communications, but to the unprogrammed simplicity by which the gospel entered there.

I'd first heard about the indigenous beginnings of the national revival while I was in Djakarta. Peter Nanfelt, director of the Christian and Missionary Alliance work in Indonesia, cited the island of Alor, which is far from the major transportation routes. There an Indonesian graduate of a CMA Bible school established his own mission in the

JAVA

★ Djakarta

● Bandung

1930s and saw it grow to more than forty congregations before his death in 1970. In nearby Timor the heralded evangelistic teams went forth, I was told, without benefit of any foreign missionaries, whose travel was restricted during the political unrest following the Communist coup attempt.

In Kesamben, East Java, the spiritual movement was accelerated by the simple quest of a teen-aged girl named Lydia—four years before the political crisis. Lydia was Muslim by registration, but like many of her fellow Javanese, she was influenced more by the spirit world of animism. She possessed a keen mind and was accepted at a high school in Kediri, about sixty miles northwest of Kesamben, in 1958. At a young people's

meeting in Kediri conducted by members of the Worldwide Evangelization Crusade, Lydia first learned about Jesus Christ. Before she completed her schooling, she accepted him as her Savior and worshiped regularly with the Kediri Christians.

Lydia missed this fellowship keenly when she returned to Kesamben in 1961. The only Christian believer in her community of 9,000 people, Lydia couldn't keep her faith to herself. She spoke to her parents about Jesus Christ, but her father angrily silenced her. She continued to speak to others, however, and an uncle, then a girl friend, accepted the Christian faith. Though other friends did not oppose her religious deviation, their apathy toward her witnessing accentuated her desire for fellowship. She felt she needed help, but the church at Kediri was too distant to send an evangelist.

The closest Christian communion that Lydia knew about was in Malang, forty miles away, where Andrew Gih had founded the Southeast Asia Bible College. It was a school for Chinese, Lydia knew, but she wrote the college, nevertheless, urgently requesting someone to come to Kesamben and minister to the small Christian band.

Norma Jamieson of the Unevangelized Fields Mission and Lynne Newall of the Worldwide Evangelization Crusade, both Australians teaching at the school, decided to make the trip. They found a small group of people gathered to listen to the visitors, as Lydia had promised.

The first meeting indicated no fruitful ministry for the teachers. They had to speak in Indonesian, which most of the listeners could not understand. The headmaster of the primary school in Kesamben agreed to interpret for them, though he was a Muslim. He informed the visitors of his religion and added frankly: "I don't see how God can have a son."

The ladies spoke to the group about the miracles Christ performed which proved that he was more than a great man, a great teacher, or a great prophet. They spoke fervently, but they left the gathering discouraged at the lack of response.

The two instructors returned to Malang with a prayer that Lydia would be strengthened in her lonely witness, yet with very little hope that anything would come of their encounter. Two weeks later, however, the ladies received another letter from Kesamben—this one from the Muslim schoolmaster, asking them to return and begin regular meetings in his home. "Of course, we went," Miss Newall related, "but we could go only on Sunday mornings. This meant that any growth in the work would depend upon the witness of the believers." That is exactly how it was accomplished. One by one, four of the six teachers at the primary school accepted Christ and friends and neighbors were brought to the meetings.

It was hardly a rapid growth, however. At the end of six years there were still less than twenty Christian adults. But from this group five deacons were appointed for preaching and teaching. The men took their positions seriously: they prayed for opportunities to tell others about Christ, and just as they had been led to faith by the working of God's Spirit, they confidently expected the Lord to bless their witness. In this simple way people heard, came to the meetings, learned about Christ, often accepted him, and went out to tell others.

In 1968 a request came from a village

about two hours' walk up a steep mountain from Kesamben. "It didn't come to us missionaries," Miss Newall recalled. "It came to one of our Javanese deacons—'Please come and tell us about Jesus Christ.' And he went." Within two years there were two hundred Christian adults in that village!

"But not just one village wanted to hear of Christ," the missionary added. "Farther up the mountain, five hours' walk over paths that are almost impassable in the wet season, five more villages asked to hear. In all, eight new villages opened up to the gospel."

Who ministers in these villages? Not the missionaries. Rather, four local deacons. Students from the Bible college also help. As this is being written the Christian following in the Kesamben region numbers more than 3,000—and it all began with a teen-aged Indonesian girl.

In addition to the typical problems of any new congregation, the fledgling Kesamben Christians must also battle entrenched occultism. Fearsome respect is paid the *dukun,* the "witch doctor," who makes his living casting spells of good or evil. It is a good living—but not for the patrons.

A lady of the community contracted tuberculosis and suffered added shame as her husband abandoned her. To regain her health and avenge her husband's desertion, she traveled sixty miles to hire the services of a particular *dukun*. He extracted a huge payment, then uttered several incantations and gave her a special *djimat* to seal the spell. Her instructions were to toss the fetish—tied inside a bag—into a river on her way home. As instructed, she threw the *djimat* from the bus into the water without looking back. Her efforts, however, were wasted. But later she found solace and new life in the fellowship of the Kesamben believers.

Not so fortunate was the mother of one of Lydia's friends. The mother was at odds with the family next door, so she employed a *dukun* to cast spells on the neighbors. The intended victims retaliated with their own hired sorcery, and the initiator of the occult warfare died mysteriously.

Sorcery is often encountered in this island paradise. Pak Wirijantoe, pastor of Lydia's church in Kediri, received a call one day to come and pray for a fifteen-year-old Chinese girl. When he arrived with a deacon at the home, he found the girl stretched out on her bed, her eyes open but her body absolutely still. She did not respond to the pastor's words, spoken to her in Indonesian. Perplexed, Pastor Wirijantoe spoke softly to his helper in his native Javanese. To their surprise the girl suddenly sat up and started talking in Javanese, a tongue she did not normally use, and in a voice much different from her own.

"Who are you?" the bewildered pastor asked.

The name the girl uttered was not her own.

"Where do you come from?" the pastor wanted to know.

"I live at the cemetery," the voice replied.

Pak Wirijantoe prayed for wisdom. He realized the spirit speaking to him did not belong to the body it was possessing. Finally he said, "You have no right to this person. She's a Christian."

"I know that," the voice replied. "I'm not going to stay long. I came to test the children of God."

Then the girl lay down. She remained in a coma for two hours while her parents and the minister continued their prayer vigil. When she spoke at last, it was Indonesian—and in her own voice.

In the battle against witchcraft deacons play an important role as the conscience of the Kesamben church. They fearlessly denounce anyone who would put their trust in the demonic spirits, despite their obvious power. And they do their exhorting before the whole congregation.

Not only is witchcraft rebuked. A person who is too easily offended may hear a deacon's admonition to put away anger, with his name being singled out in a sermon. When a man makes a profession of faith in Christ, deacons will visit his family and may well ask the wife: "Now that your husband has professed to accept Jesus as his Savior, do you notice any difference in his life? Does he get angry at you like he used to? Is he patient with you now?"

Significantly, the reaction of those subject to this public review of their lives is generally one of meekness. How have the deacons attained such respect? The answer I was given to this question by a Western missionary who has frequently visited this indigenous church is a study in simplicity, yet a pattern for any disciple of Christ: "They are recognized for the fact that they *know* the gospel—and are sharing it."

5

The School on Fire

Not far from Kesamben is a small Bible school whose contribution to the Indonesian revival is incalculable. The Indonesian Bible Institute at Batu has provided the spiritual catalyst for igniting revival fires throughout the islands, including Timor's blaze.

Situated in a high valley amid Java's lushly garbed volcanic mountains, the Indonesian Bible Institute enjoys a picturesque setting. It was founded in Batu by Heini and Agnes Germann-Edey, literature and radio missionaries serving with Worldwide Evangelization Crusade. When the Institute opened in 1959, nine enrolling students were greeted by an international teaching staff of four, including the Swiss (Heini) and Canadian (Agnes) founders, an Australian (Gwen Fredericks), and a German (Detmar Scheunemann).

In 1961 the Germann-Edeys left to work with U. S.-based World Vision, and Indonesians trained at the Institute formed a national board which took over operation of the school, with Scheunemann remaining as principal. The staff has remained multinational, with Asians, Europeans, New Zealanders, and Americans living and working with Indonesians. Students, too, represent a variety of backgrounds, coming from all parts of the island republic.

The outstanding characteristic of the Institute is not its ethnic mixture, however. Permeating the campus is a discernable atmosphere of joyful love. It can be seen in the smiles that spread spontaneously across youthful faces. It can be sensed in the harmonious singing that starts every morning in a chapel service soon after the 4:00 A.M. rising gong and is renewed throughout the day in classroom devotional periods. It can be felt in every contact with the people who make up the Batu Bible institute.

I relished sessions around the table of Volkhardt Scheunemann, Delmar's brother and an instructor in the school, who with his effervescent wife Gerlinde invited students and staff to share meals and fellowship with me. Casually mentioning on one occasion my need of an airmail envelope, I soon had a dozen. When Volkhardt learned after my arrival that I was not accustomed to travel in

Indonesia, he quickly supplied me with soap and towel, items not generally installed in the simple bathroom facilities of rural areas, and a flashlight to guide my evening's walk to my room since the campus community lacked electric illumination.

It is in such a spirit of loving concern, I discovered, that the school's policies have been established. In order to insure individualized attention for students, enrollment has been kept small in spite of the demand for education in Indonesia. It was only in 1970 that the student body exceeded one hundred. With the establishment in 1965 of a Bible school in Tandjung Enim, Sumatra, and in 1968 of a sister school in Soé, Timor— the one headed by Sardjito Martosudarmo— the Institute's outreach has been further expanded.

Students are presented with a strong emphasis on evangelism in all of their training which, surprisingly enough for Batu's remote location, may include radio production. Seizing upon the high interest in radio spawned by the appearance of inexpensive transistor models and the abundance of amateur radio stations operating under easily-obtained broadcast licenses, the Institute has equipped its own recording studio. Students work with a British staff member, Ernie Shingler, in preparing tapes of "Sing, My Heart," a music program with Bible readings which is broadcast over a dozen Indonesian stations.

But personal evangelism remains the key to the school's mission outreach. The training starts with weekend trips to surrounding villages. Students may later join longer excursions to other islands as members of the school's renowned evangelistic teams.

The financial requirements for these excursions, as for other Institute ventures, are never publicized. Staff members and students rely directly on God to supply the needed funds. Gifts from contributors—sixty percent Indonesian, forty percent foreign—have always proved adequate. The same expectant attitude applies to the school's evangelistic endeavors, which have touched every major island in Indonesia. "We go only to areas where we are invited," Detmar Scheunemann told me. How do they gain invitations to achieve their wide outreach? "We pray them in," he said.

The unusual response to the school's efforts has been a surprise to Institute leaders even though, according to Scheunemann, "We started to pray for revival in Indonesia at the establishment of the Bible Institute." One of the great obstacles to evangelism encountered by the students was occult power. Black magic and white magic are practiced throughout the islands, Detmar told me.

He explained the difference: black magic is

used for passing a bad spirit onto a person; white magic is used for "good" purposes, such as healing. In white magic the name of the Trinity is sometimes invoked, along with using formulas derived from the *Sixth and Seventh Books of Moses,* a notorious sorcery manual. It is clear, however, that the diviners and their subjects place their faith not in God but in the magic forces.

"If one is healed by this means," Detmar said, "the devil has a right to that person. He seldom comes to spiritual rebirth. He may fall asleep in the church services or react in a violent way. If the blood of Christ is mentioned, the possessed individual may even attack the speaker."

"How do you minister to someone like this?" I wanted to know.

"We have to use the apostolic ways of casting out evil spirits. Our formula comes from the New Testament. In some cases we have had to have several people uniting together in prayer and fasting to expel a spirit."

"Have you ever been confronted by someone possessed?" I asked.

"Oh, many times," he replied, and then related several instances. One was particularly intriguing:

Addressing a group on the small southern island of Roti, Detmar was talking about the spiritual development of King Saul, who at one point contacted demonic powers (1 Sam-

The map behind Detmar Scheunemann, principal of the Indonesian Bible Institute, shows outreach of his students throughout the island republic.

uel 28). Suddenly a listener jumped from his seat with a wild cry and started toward the pulpit. The startled congregation stirred but made no move to stop the man. Detmar learned later that the people were desperately afraid of the person who was known as one possessed by ninety-nine spirits and seeking one more.

"You cannot do anything in this room!" Detmar shouted to the man as he advanced menacingly up the aisle. "In the name of Jesus, sit down!"

As Detmar voiced the name of Jesus, the attacker fell to the floor. Students from the Batu team carried him to the rear of the church, where they and the local pastor ministered to him as the sermon continued. That night the man was relieved of the many demons who had ruled him.

The following evening in front of the astonished congregation, the man openly confessed his faith in Christ and described how he had been delivered one by one of the evil spirits that he harbored. Through his testimony, many in the audience were drawn to an acceptance of Christ or a recommitment of their lives to him.

Scheunemann's words seemed unnatural to me, coming as they did from a staid German Lutheran. His delivery was extremely matter-of-fact and convincing, even when he described the amazing way that the school's mission sights were raised beyond Indonesia.

At the 1965 conference of the Indonesian Missionary Fellowship, the school-sponsored mission agency, an official of Worldwide Evangelization Crusade presented statistics on mission needs around the world. The IMF conferees were impressed, but they felt their hands were full with the work that had to be done in Indonesia. The following day, however, Institute President Petrus Octavianus told the group about a vision during the night.

As he was praying about the staggering mission needs around the world, Octavianus reported, his spirit was separated from his body and transported over the countries of Malaysia, Cambodia, and Thailand; and he had a tremendous desire to take the Christian message to the people of Southeast Asia. Afterward, his spirit reunited with his body, he prayed for these people in the tongues of the countries which his spirit had seen. Speaking in an unknown tongue was new to him—in fact, this phenomenon was rarely reported to me in connection with the Indonesian revival. But through Octavianus' report a decision was made to launch an outreach to Southeast Asia. The IMF formed plans—only to see them engulfed by the political upheaval and Communist bloodbath that followed.

Not until 1968 did Octavianus lead the first IMF team outside Indonesia. The group traveled up the Malay Penninsula to Thailand and Cambodia, where they encouraged Christian converts left adrift by government ouster of Western missionaries. In later journeys IMF teams took their message to Pakistan, the divided Islamic state bordering India, and to Japan.

By spiritual standards, the IMF leadership is notable, as I ascertained from one firsthand report: "Pak" (an Indonesian title of respect) Octavianus had traveled to a small West Irian village in the spring of 1970 for a conference of churches. It was not a pretentious site. There wasn't a building in the area large enough to hold the scores in attendance . . . living accommodations were minimal, the villagers sharing their homes with the delegates . . . transportaion to the place was as unpredictable as the end-of-the-rainy-season weather. But the village was centrally located and the people, who weren't accustomed to luxury anyway, gladly sacrificed some comforts to attend the meeting. It marked a new era of independence for the church in West Irian, the western half of the New Guinea island which became a part of Indonesia in 1963.

Conference planners had expectantly asked God's blessing on the gathering; not even a threatening sky could quench their exuberance at the large company of Christians who assembled in a clearing for the opening session. But before the first word was spoken, rain burst down upon them.

From a hurried huddle on the speakers' platform, the short, bespectacled Octavianus stepped quickly to the rostrum and shouted,

Indonesian evangelistic leader Petrus Octavianus enjoys reunion with his family after a speaking tour. (Photo by David Mitchell)

"Let us pray!" His authoritative voice stopped the spontaneous flight to cover. "Lord," the man called out, "you know these people have traveled far to come together in your name. Don't let them be disappointed." The speaker stretched his hand out toward the crowd and shouted, "In the name of Jesus, the rain should stop!"

Conference leaders who had prayed that the Holy Spirit would permeate the gathering were astonished when the heavy rain stopped abruptly at the command given in Jesus' name. They needed no further proof of

God's presence; all the following sessions seemed infused with spiritual fire, undampened by rain.

The man who had called on God to still the storm is an unpretentious father of seven whose name one hears frequently among Indonesian Christian circles. Pak Octavianus has spent most of his adult life as an educator. At thirty he was the principal of a teachers college in Malang, East Java. He was also an elder in a local Protestant church, but, according to his own testimony, he lacked the new birth experience until he was confronted with this need at an evangelistic meeting.

Soon afterward, Octavianus started holding after-class Bible studies for the college students. And every school term from thirty to forty Muslims were converted to Christianity, while Christians were inspired to deeper consecration. Octavianus felt that God wanted him to do more, and in 1960 he overrode the objections of friends and family to enroll in the one-year-old Indonesian Bible Institute in nearby Batu. As he trained and later taught at the Institute, Octavianus was to see the small school carry spiritual fire to outlying islands, and eventually to foreign lands.

This foreign outreach is yet merely flickering. But then it was an apparently insignificant spark that set Timor ablaze.

6

Rugged Road to Bali

It was a long day and a half.

I arose at four o'clock Saturday morning in Batu, East Java, and didn't sink into bed again until half past one Sunday afternoon in Denpasar on the fabled isle of Bali. The journey—a distance of less than 300 miles—was made of necessity in an auto, a bus, a ferry, and a pickup truck, with long waits between conveyances. By the time the journey was completed, however, I'd gotten a close look at life in Indonesia and I could better appreciate the miracle of a widespread spiritual revival in a country so meagerly endowed with transportation and communication facilities.

I couldn't help but compare Indonesia's evangelistic prospects with America's, where

Christian groups rely heavily on rapid transportation and instant communication to accomplish their goals. Try to imagine a large American crusade—or even a congregational campaign—without the help of a telephone, the postal service, news media, and automobile—if not jet—transportation. These tools are rarely available to Indonesian churches. And yet the revival is there.

A few days before my tiresome journey to Bali I left Djakarta by jet to reach Surabaja, East Java, where I took a *bemo* to Batu in the mountains. A *bemo* is Indonesia's answer to the need for inexpensive, short-distance transportation. It is a small panel truck or covered pickup converted to a passenger carrier with benches on either side of the cargo area. In Batu, at the Indonesian Bible Institute, I was introduced to the tropical practice of rising early. The gong that awakens students at 4:00 A.M. is loud and compelling. Unlike myself, the Batu students were able to sing at that hour—and spiritedly. Their joyous music was still ringing in my ears after breakfast as I was driven by car down the macadam road on my return trip to Surabaja.

The road was already crowded with Javanese villagers starting their day's work. Men and boys were carrying balanced loads of rice shocks or other produce on the ends of their *pikuls,* the poles they port across their shoulders. Some guided oxen that pulled carts loaded with huge bamboo poles or other massive cargo. A few were leading goats or herding ducks to market, the latter by holding a bamboo stick before the loudly squawking birds which are trained to follow a cloth flapping at the pole's end. Women walked gracefully along, balancing big bundles of garden produce atop their heads. Girls packed their baby brothers or sisters in shoulder slings and, with the younger boys, herded smaller siblings along behind their parents.

Though a variety of products were represented in the market parade, the roadside scenery attested to Indonesia's rice economy. All stages of rice production—from the planting in the paddies to the cutting and winnowing—could be observed, thanks to the long growing season in the equatorial climate. And yet insufficient rice is grown locally to feed the teeming population. It must be purchased from countries such as the United States and Australia which produce enough to export.

Not one of the multitude on the road, I was certain, owned an automobile, a telephone, or a television set, although some may have possessed transistor radios. But I was struck by the apparent happiness of the people as they walked and talked together. Though physically burdened with their market products, none seemed to be weighed down with worries, if their cheerful countenances provided an accurate barometer.

As we came into the outskirts of Surabaja, *betjak* drivers with their jingling bell "horns" and food vendors with their "tink-tonk" call to customers added their number to the procession. I looked with more compassion this time on the *betjak* drivers, who had seemed a bit too raucous in their competition for customers outside the Hotel Indonesia in Djakarta. For I had seen them in a different pose on my wee-hour ride to the airport a few days earlier. The homeless entrepreneurs had been curled in their passenger seats or sprawled on the road beside their cycles, trying to catch a little sleep before their long day's work would begin again.

I was dropped off at the Willard Stone residence in Surabaja. Stone operates a Christian Literature Crusade bookstore in this large East Java port. The two of us attempted to secure air passage for me to Denpasar, where I was to contact a missionary working among Bali's Hindu population and also catch a Monday flight to Timor. Even with two airlines servicing Denpasar, the combined schedule did not offer daily flights as an American traveler might expect. I couldn't get to Denpasar by air until Monday, which meant I'd miss my connection to Timor and also lose valuable days from my precise itinerary. The solution was to take the bus. We found I could get an overnight run leaving at 9:30 that evening.

Before my departure the Stones supplied me with pillows, a large thermos of tea, and some important Indonesian phrases to help me get food, drink, or find the "W.C." ("way-say" in Indonesian). Rest stops with meals or refreshments were part of the ticket price, which was ridiculously inexpensive compared to American fares. But then my Lilliputian bus to Bali was hardly an air-conditioned Greyhound. It was built for Orientals much smaller in stature than Americans. Its luggage space was inadequate for the amount everyone wanted to bring along. Bags and boxes were above us, beneath us, and in the aisle. Fortunately, I was near the door, with only a couple of cases to step over. I was also fortunate enough to get a place on the two-seat side of the aisle instead of the three-seat side, but I didn't get the window seat.

Willard had forewarned me that the islanders had an aversion to night air and that all the windows would probably be closed. I managed to convince my youthful seat partner to keep ours open a crack, which perhaps gave some psychological relief to the stuffy enclosure. I asked my companion, who appeared to be no more than twenty, if he could speak English. He smiled and nodded affirmatively, but my ensuing rush of words was obviously unintelligible to him. I had already discovered that these very agreeable people hate to tell anyone "no." My limited command of Indonesian did not permit a lively conversation, especially on a cramped nighttime bus ride; so, except for facial expressions to indicate our mutual discomfort or amusement over some passenger's prank, communication between my seat companion and myself was virtually nil throughout the fifteen-hour trip.

In silence, then, I settled down to feel more than slightly sorry for myself. Why—in our supposedly modern, technological world— should I be stuck with such slow, hot, and uncomfortable transportation? The Stones' pillows were a boon, but I could never get my feet adjusted satisfactorily on top of my flight bag—or if I did find a relatively comfortable position, the bus would reach a rest stop and I'd have to get up to let my partner out—so I slept very little through the night. I spent most of the trip sipping tea and silently "singing" hymns to take my thoughts away from my aching bones.

My introspective woe was a distinct contrast to the ever-contented acceptance of life's hardships that my fellow Indonesian travelers displayed. While I chafed impatiently at the discomfort and the slowness of the outmoded transportation, they talked animatedly—or slept peacefully—and were always ready to give their Western guest an encouraging smile. Getting there *now* was not an imperative with them. "Perhaps tomorrow," a phrase I heard frequently in Indonesia whenever I asked the time of an event, was more than a vague, placating answer. It typified a philosophy of life that recognizes the inevitability of hardships but refuses to be shaken by them.

It was four o'clock Sunday morning when we reached Banjuwangi on the eastern tip of Java. Stone had told me that if we didn't make the 6:00 A.M. ferry to Bali, we'd have at least a three-hour wait for the next circuit. We lost the "race." Several buses were ahead of us when we arrived at the landing and ours didn't make the ferry until its second run at 9:30. In the meantime we watched the sun rise over the Bali Straits, had breakfast, and waited.

I spent some of the time reading from the pocket *Living New Testament* which my publisher, Ken Taylor, the paraphraser, had given me before the trip. I was amazed at how the Scriptures, particularly this version, seemed to describe the things that are happening now in Indonesia.

In John's Gospel I read Christ's prophetic words: "In solemn truth I tell you, anyone believing in me shall do the same miracles I have done, and even greater ones" (14:12).

Was this the key to the spiritual fruit that this country had witnessed? A belief—a strong and trusting belief—that God would act today through his servants as he did through his Son?

I tried to project such a trust within my circumstances. Could I successfully use Christ's name to effect a miracle like those reported on these islands? I knew that I could not rid myself of a shadow of doubt about a supernatural event being possible. My very culture precluded it. And yet, what were Jesus' instructions when he sent out his disciples: "Heal the sick, raise the dead, cure the lepers, and cast out demons" (Matthew 10:8). Faith healing, demon purging, and resurrections from the dead are all a part of the religious phenomena of Indonesia.

I reread Luke's parallel account, which records the disciples' astonishment at their ability to perform mighty acts in Jesus' name, and was impressed at the Lord's reply to their amazement: " 'The important thing is not that demons obey you, but that your names are registered as citizens of heaven.' Then he was filled with the joy of the Holy Spirit and said, 'I praise you, O Father, Lord of heaven and earth, for hiding these things from the intellectuals and worldly wise and for revealing them to those who are as trusting as little children' " (Luke 10:20, 21).

That was a good description of the Indonesian Christians' faith.

As I was meditating on these passages, a Chinese passenger on the bus came to the bench I was sitting on and said in English, "I see we're both reading from the Word this morning." I looked up. He held an open Indonesian Testament in his hand. I invited him to sit beside me. We shared the inspiration we'd each received from our reading that morning. It was an unexpected blessing, on a trip that had been long and wearisome, to be able to have this fellowship with a fellow believer.

The rest of the journey was bearable. I never could find a comfortable spot for my feet, and I sweltered from the heat in the stuffy bus, which was intensified by the tropical sun arcing above us; but there was so much to see! As the ferry pulled out of Banjuwangi across the peacock-blue water, its passengers were granted a breathtaking view of the eastern Java coast. A palm-tree-lined beach stretched for miles before a rising verdant hillside that led to distant volcanic mountains, which in turn were poking their cones above fleecy, low-hanging clouds.

In Bali there were numerous mountain streams spanned by narrow bridges; the strange, boar-like pigs which abound in this Hindu land where, unlike Muslim areas, pork is "kosher"; and the many pagoda-like family shrines with gargoyles and statues of the fearsome Hindu gods. And there were the

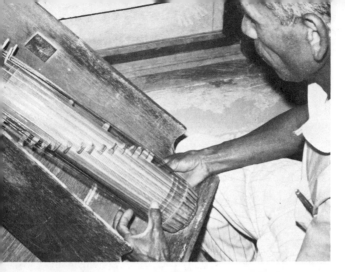

This Timorese musical instrument, called a susandu, *produces a harpsichord sound. It is played by plucking the strings which are placed around a cylindrical core.*

people: beautiful, bronze-skinned children splashing in the streams; smiling men and women in their colorful sarongs. As we neared Denpasar, their number increased. They were walking on the roadsides, cycling down the streets, crowding into *bemos,* and overflowing the beds of cargo trucks.

Boys and *bemos* were waiting at our bus stop, the youngsters boarding the bus to gain a luggage-carrying tip before the passengers could even debark. Two boys latched onto the American, beaming at their "catch," no doubt hopeful of a generous gratuity. The older one, who spoke a little English, inquired if I wanted a hotel. "No," I told him, explaining as best I could that I had a contact in Denpasar and wanted only to get to a telephone. He insisted there was no telephone in the area. I looked around desperately for my Chinese friend; but he had already disappeared, as, strangely, most of the other passengers had, too. There seemed to be only myself, the empty bus, the two boys, and a waiting *bemo* in the bus lot.

Assured by the older boy that he would get me to a telephone, I reluctantly boarded the pickup-truck *bemo*. We had not gone far before my guide indicated our stop was next. I paid the driver and the boys grabbed my two bags. We were at a fashionable hotel, obviously designed for the tourist trade. Here English was readily understood. "I'm sorry, but we are filled today," the man at the desk told me after I'd followed the boys into the hotel. I joined the man in an appraisal of my wrinkled and sweat-stained clothing and self-consciously rubbed my day-old beard. I decided that this was not a hint for a bribe as I had been told might happen; this man really didn't want me to stay in his fancy hotel. I asked if I could use a telephone and was granted this request. I checked my notebook for the number I'd been given and dialed.

There was no answer.

Outside the hotel my young guide told me confidently that he could get me into another place not far away. He spoke to his companion in Indonesian and the two started off with my luggage. A long block down the road the boys turned into a side street and led me another block to a more-Indonesian-looking stucco building with the name "Damai" painted above the door. I found out later that the name meant "Peace," but I was far from peaceful at that moment. The manager could barely speak English, just enough to let me know that he had a vacant room and could get me to the airport in time for my flight out the next day.

Before he showed me the room, I asked to use the telephone. I tried again to reach my Denpasar contact, but as before there was no answer. Subsequent attempts that day were equally futile. Only later, on another Bali stop, did I learn that the missionary and his wife were out of town for the day. Word of my coming had failed to reach them through the uncertain mail system. Resignedly, I followed the hotel manager to the room. It was hardly a luxury suite, but it did have its own bath, such as it was; and I was hot, tired, and ready to drop almost anywhere. I took it. The boys brought in my luggage and I paid them for their excellent service. They left, their faces glowing. The manager bowed out and I sat down on the bed to consider my next move.

I felt utterly desolate. This was the first time during my Indonesian visit that I had missed making a scheduled connection. Now I was all alone in a strange place. Alone and miserable. The oppressive temperature in the non-air-conditioned room was little better than on the bus. My clammy clothes clung to my fervid body. How could anyone stand to live in this lousy climate, I wondered. But I was really too weary to speculate on the unlikely contentment of the island people or why God had permitted this ordeal to happen to me. The watch on my sweat-beaded arm told me it was 1:30 in the afternoon. It was time for the *tengah-hari* rest and I was ready for it.

But not before I shed the dirty clothes and grimy sweat sticking to my skin. Begrudging the fact that there was no shower in the bathroom, I lathered up with my soap and unheated water from the vat that occupied one corner of the dingy closet. Until the moment that followed, when I let the first dipperful of cool water splash down over me, I really hadn't appreciated the pure pleasure of an Indonesian dip bath. Had I not shared briefly the austere life of the islanders, I could not have understood the importance of such a seemingly simple blessing. Nor would I have stood in such awe at God's mighty work among these people. It was a miniature revival for my spirit.

Repeatedly I dipped the refreshing liquid over my feverish body. It was glorious!

7

Dreams, Demons, and Dedication

"We don't have a revival here in Sulawesi; we *need* one."

That was the blunt assessment of Maurice Bliss, instructor at the Jaffray School of Theology in Makassar, when I asked about spiritual conditions in this island better known in the West as "Celebes." His tongue-in-cheek pessimism was based on Sulawesi's relatively small increase in church membership, but God's Spirit has nonetheless been active on this island.

Religion-wise, Sulawesi appears to be a microcosm of all Indonesia. The Dutch colonists tried to regulate religious development by giving preference to specific faiths where they predominated. Islam, which came to the area in the 1500s, received the greatest preference as the majority religion; Hindus were granted precedence in Bali; the Catholics got Flores; Protestants could enter Dutch Timor; Borneo was limited largely to native religions—to cite a few examples. But Sulawesi, with its international port of Makassar, was a haven for almost all of the islands' religious groups. Religious faith, however, cannot be legislated—particularly the kind spread by the Holy Spirit. This was illustrated vividly to me shortly after a Dutch missionary told me flatly that he did not believe there could be a true convert from Islam.

Max, a former Muslim, gave me a singular account of his conversion. While contrasting sharply with other biblically-oriented Christian activity in Sulawesi, his story demonstrates the extent of mystical influence in Indonesia.

In a dream Max saw himself pulling a bell rope in a Christian church. This was particularly unnerving because he had never been inside or even around a church. He was from a strict Muslim family. His father, in fact, was a teacher of the Koran.

No matter how he tried, Max could not forget his dream. Finally, in desperation, he paid a visit to the local Christian pastor and told him about it.

"The Lord was speaking to you through your dream," the pastor told Max. "He wants you to become a Christian."

"Impossible!" was Max's spontaneous reac-

At typical Indonesian market—this one is in Kupang, Timor—customers buy and use produce quickly before it wilts in the tropical heat.

tion. But how else to explain the dream?

"Will you at least study the Christian faith?" the pastor invited.

Max agreed. As he read the New Testament, he was gripped with the unshakable conviction that this was the truth. After earnest conversation and prayer with the pastor, Max made his decision to be baptized. He knew full well the danger such an act could mean in his strongly Islamic community, but he looked for protection to his newfound Savior. Max found Christ completely worthy of such trust. Today the one-time Muslim is busy bringing other followers of Islam to Christ.

Much different from Max's account was a solemn report I received from Peter Anggu, assistant pastor of a church in Makassar and a part-time faculty member of the Jaffray School. The young preacher was raised by animistic grandparents but became a Christian through the witness of his father with whom he was reunited at the age of ten.

Anggu's early life was entwined in the worship of spirits, for his grandfather was an animist priest in the largely animist province of Toradja. When the rice was just poking its head through the water in the paddies, Peter knew it was time for his grandfather to offer the bloody chicken sacrifices so that the field would produce much grain. At harvest time he would see his grandfather sacrifice a water buffalo as a thank-offering—or, if the harvest was meager, to appease the spirits who controlled the crop. Peter would sometimes accompany his grandfather when the old man would try to make a sick person well with his various methods of conjuration. Life seemed to be a weird game of pleasing capricious spirits.

When the youth rejoined his parents, he stepped into an entirely different life. His father, among the few in the area who had become Christian, trusted a single God to supply all his needs. There was no anxiety about the whims of fickle spirits. "It seems in my father's home we were always happy," Mr. Anggu recalled. "There was real joy and peace." Peter's father was a simple, uneducated man who had completed only one year of school. Yet Peter, who enjoyed public schooling under the new government's policy of compulsory education, was impressed by his father's ability to read the Bible. "Even today he reads his Bible although it is hard for him to read other things," Mr. Anggu told me.

In the late 1940s the faith of Peter's parents was severely tested when a fanatic Islamic movement sprang up to force people to become Muslims. The Anggus' village was on the edge of Toradja, which was a prime target of the Muslim advance. Zealous Muslims entered the village many times to oppress the people, threatening physical harm if they resisted conversion, and sometimes carrying it out. Christian churches were burned, only to be rebuilt by the persevering believers.

One Toradjanese Christian was seized by the fanatics and tortured. He was even made to dig his own grave, but he refused to renounce his faith in Christ. Before he could be executed, he escaped "because of our people's prayers," Mr. Anggu reported. The border village was able to resist the Muslim onslaught and protect the rest of the area.

Mr. Anggu's father and the other Christians of the Toradja villages were products of Indonesian evangelism, largely members of the "Kibaid" church, which has its roots in World War II. When the Japanese occupied the East Indies, the pastor of a church in Makassar, Rev. Bokko', went back to his native Toradja, where he was forced to stay. Unable to return to his own congregation, he began a new ministry of evangelism where he was. Two things marked Mr. Bokko's work among the villagers: Spirit-filled songs, which attracted Toradja's natural-born singers; and an emphasis on Bible reading. The villagers were intrigued by the opportunity to add new songs to a vast repertoire which stretched back into their ancestry. Mr. Bokko' himself possessed a love of singing and seemed to communicate his love of God best through song.

Once gathered for a songfest, villagers were eager to participate. Would they like to learn a new song? They would. Did they understand the song's meaning? For the many who did not, Bokko' used the opportunity to explain the Christian message behind the words. Gospel singing coupled with Rev. Bokko's explanation of the message brought many animists to faith in Christ. To ground them in their new faith, Mr. Bokko' encouraged Bible reading.

By war's end Mr. Bokko' had established a sizable "congregation" scattered among the Toradja villages. Some of his followers came from the ranks of nominal Christians, products of the original Dutch partitioning, but most were converted from animism. Peter Anggu's father was one of the latter.

To nurture the new Christians, Mr. Bokko' decided to stay in Toradja after the war and train young evangelists to minister to the village groups. In 1953 Peter Anggu, who had accepted his father's enthusiastic Christianity, became a member of Mr. Bokko's third class of evangelist trainees.

Though now advanced in age, Mr. Bokko' still ministers to his large body of Toradja followers. He still walks throughout the area and continues to inspire young evangelists. He receives support for his work from Peter Anggu's church in Makassar, which is pastored by one of Rev. Bokko's Toradja colleagues, Rev. Lalang.

Compared to the large expansion of Christianity on other Indonesian islands, the Kibaid Church membership in the mere tens of thousands, may seem insignificant. It has become second in size, however, to the church established by early Dutch missionaries in this remote mountain province of only 400,000 people, over half of whom are still unreached by any organized religion. And Rev. Bokko's Bible-and-hymnbook evangelism is steadily changing those statistics.

With the diversity of spiritual activity which I encountered in Sulawesi, it was not surprising for me to meet in Makassar an individual whose Christian experience represents a compatible fusion of charismatic power and more conventional evangelism. She was a shy, seventeen-year-old student at the Jaffray school who had come from Sumba, one of Indonesia's southernmost islands lying between Java and Timor.

Mada had been reared by Christian parents in the "Kemah Indjil" Church established by the Christian and Missionary Alliance. She was a young teen-ager enrolled in a teacher-preparation school in her home town of Kambaniru when, in her words, she was "born spiritually." This happened, she said, during evangelistic meetings held in her local church by "Team 36" from Soé.

Once again, as Mada spoke through an interpreter, I realized I had encountered an indirect product of the Timorese revival, a situation that occurred on many of the islands I visited. The Batu and Soé evangelistic teams, so numerous they were identified by number, have spiritual fruit throughout Indonesia. Typically, at Kambaniru, the team leaders emphasized that their listeners should forget the names of the team members and remember only what the Lord had done. The speaker for Team 36 was an eloquent youth who effectively used Bible references to impress his listeners with God's attitude toward sin, especially the sin of witchcraft which is a way of life on the islands.

In my interview with Mada I also became aware of the demonic power of witchcraft and the important role that fear plays in maintaining its hold over the islanders. During the interview I mentioned to our interpreter, Canadian Gordon Chapman, an instructor in the Jaffray school, an incident that had happened to me in Timor. I recalled the distressed look that had appeared on the face of my host in Soé when I'd asked about photographing a fetish. He had told me emphatically that the *djimats* were always destroyed when their possession was confessed. Gordon then described the awesome respect which the island people accord the *djimat* spirits.

A fetish—which may be any object from an

Fetishes, such as these roots, cords, and stones surrendered by new Christian converts, must be destroyed to protect former owners from the evil spirits which inhabit them. The djimats, *sometimes placed in pouches (upper left), are worn hidden under clothing to give the possessor special powers. (Photo by Gordon Chapman)*

ancestral knife to a root or stone concealed about the body—is considered the residence of a powerful spirit which can be called upon by the bearer in time of need or when he desires to excel in a supernatural way. The spirits must be treated carefully, for they are thought to control life and death. For many islanders the fear of the spirits' retaliation stands in the way of their relinquishing *djimats* to become trusting Christians. When fetishes are confessed, they are burned in a special ceremony which includes prayers for the protection of the bearer from retaliation by the evil spirit.

Ask an islander if he still believes in the spirit's power after the *djimat* is burned, and he will quickly tell you he does indeed. As a Christian, however, he relies on God's far greater power to protect him from the many manifestations that evil can take.

The islanders' fear of demonic reaction is based on more than superstition. Gordon told me of a missionary who rescued some fetishes from a burning to take home on furlough. Before he could use any of them in his speaking engagements, however, one of his children fell deathly ill. Prayers and medical help seemed to do no good. Finally the missionary realized the sickness might have something to do with the fetishes. Reluctantly, he destroyed the valuable lecture tools, and immediately the child recovered.

Because of the grip exerted by witchcraft, the evangelistic team in Kambaniru stressed God's power to release its hold. The Sumbanese attending the meetings were amazed at the large number of people revealing their *djimats* and releasing them for burning. One man who had surrendered a number of fetishes still seemed distraught. Then, as the team leaders and church members prayed that he be relieved of his reliance on fetishes, he relinquished still others. When all the *djimats* had been surrendered he received the peace he sought. Mada marveled as his worried visage was transformed to one of tranquility.

During the ten days of meetings, Mada became increasingly aware of the failings in her own life, but she did not care to admit them publicly. What she was witnessing impressed her, but she resisted invitations given by the team to come forward in an act of commitment to Christ.

On the last three days of their visit the team leaders gave an opportunity for any in the audience who cared to be healed from physical or spiritual illnesses to come forward. The speaker carefully explained that it was not the team but God alone who would perform the act of healing. Mada could not deny God's power when she saw the miracles, including the return to normal size of the enlarged neck of a lady who suffered from a goiter and the healing of both her parents from sicknesses that had kept them from their daily routines. Ashamed of her reluctance to trust in God's power, Mada at last went to the altar to dedicate her life to serving Christ.

I found Mada's way of expressing her experience particularly meaningful, having myself "suffered" Indonesia's heat. "After I confessed my sins and received God's forgiveness," she said. "I felt good, as if I had taken a cool bath on a hot day."

After the meetings Mada was surprised at her boldness in joining other young people in

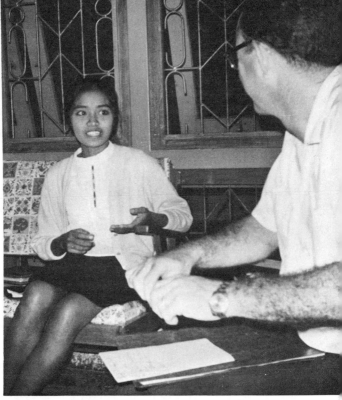

"Where will I be witnessing tomorrow?" young Sumbanese evangelist Mada ponders in conversation with Gordon Chapman, one of her instructors at the Jaffray School of Theology.

sharing her faith with inmates of a government prison in Kambaniru. When she finished her teacher-preparation course and began teaching in another community, she enlisted the help of two fellow teachers in telling the people in villages surrounding the school about Christ. Despite her active Christian witness, Mada felt pulled toward full-time

Christian service. She continued teaching, however, "until the day God dealt with me." On her way to school one morning she twisted her ankle and fell to the ground. Mada was certain the Lord was reminding her she had not made definite plans to enter Christian work. She asked God's forgiveness and renewed her vow to make plans to gain a Christian education. Relieved of her pain, she walked on to school.

That evening she returned to Kambaniru for a midweek prayer meeting. Early the next morning, only half awake, she thought she heard a voice tell her, "If you are an office worker in this world, become my disciple." This roused her. Then she heard another statement from the same voice. "If you are a teacher, leave it and be my disciple." Completely awake, she got out of bed and prayed, "If this is the devil, deliver me from him, Lord." No matter how hard she prayed, the impression that God had called her to his service did not diminish; instead it increased. That week she applied for admission to the Jaffray school, and she was soon on her way to Makassar.

She concluded our interview by telling me: "Tomorrow I will be three years old spiritually. I wonder where I will be witnessing."

With an evangelistic spirit like that among Christians on Sulawesi, the revival the island "needs" may not be long in coming.

8

Surging Life on Sumatra

It took two long jet flights to get me from Sulawesi to North Sumatra. One was across nearly a thousand miles of ocean, to Djakarta, West Java. The other was of equal distance across only two-thirds of Indonesia's giant island, Sumatra.

One can visualize the importance of this vast island by a glance at a map. Its nearly 200,000 square miles make it the sixth largest island in the world, Indonesia's second largest land mass, and the republic's largest wholly owned island. Besides its geographic consequence and attendant political and economic importance, its contribution to the recent religious history of Indonesia has likewise been significant. It was in North Sumatra that large-scale conversion to Christianity from animism gained world attention in

1964—a full year before the Communist bloodbath made the country religion-conscious. Since that time unexpected Christian inroads have been achieved into Muslim areas of Sumatra as well.

I learned about some of these remarkable Christian advances while I was still in Java. Detmar Scheunemann of the Indonesian Bible Institute in Batu mentioned several instances of the school's students or graduates penetrating Muslim fortresses in Sumatra. Their outreach includes Atjeh territory in the far north and Serawai territory in the south, considered among the most fanatic Muslim areas in Indonesia. Of Scheunemann's carefully detailed examples, the following best illustrates God's mysterious work on Sumatra.

Before 1964 conversions from Islam to Christianity in this area were virtually nil. The few Christians in the Muslim regions had moved there from other islands, brought in as government employees or plantation workers, or were among the ubiquitous Chinese merchants who are dispersed throughout East Asia. Worldwide Evangelization Crusade missionaries entered South Sumatra in 1953 and established a ministry among the migrants, but they were unable to overcome local Muslim resistance to Christianity. The WEC workers had not forsaken prayer for the Muslim population, nevertheless.

In 1963 an answer to this decade of prayer came from a surprising source: Communism. At Christmastime that year one of the leaders of the Serawai tribe, a younger-generation Muslim who believed that he could serve both Islam and Communism, attended a Communist indoctrination course in Bengkulu. The young man was disheartened at the obviously atheistic stance of Communism, however, and he left the gathering in a state of inner turmoil. While still in Bengkulu he saw an automobile parked near a church with the word "Indjil" printed on it. He recognized the connection of this word for "gospel" with Christianity—but he felt drawn to it. He walked to the car, not knowing that it belonged to a WEC missionary who was preaching a Christmas sermon inside the church. Through an open window he could hear the message of peace, and it appealed to him more than the call to revolution he had received at the Communist gathering.

He would never forget what he heard that day about God's Son come to earth. Carrying the message home with him, he told his friends about the strange but comforting words of God's forgiveness of sins. He yearned to learn more about this God of love, but how could he? In desperation one day he wrote out his request in a letter and addressed it simply to "Indjil, Bengkulu."

Amazingly, the inadequately-labeled letter

was delivered—to a retired government worker who was now the leader of a Bengkulu congregation. Frederick Tobing could scarcely believe what he was reading: a Muslim wanting to know more about Christ. Early in 1964 he visited the troubled inquirer and was surprised to be received warmly by the whole community. The Muslims he had known previously had made it a point to avoid close contact with Christians. But these people, primed by their young leader's enthusiasm, wanted to hear more about God's Son. Tobing was able to preach openly, even in the Muslim community's mosque. With this unexpected new ministry, he was thankful for the training he had received, after his retirement, at the Batu Bible institute.

In March Pak Tobing returned to Batu to attend a conference of the Indonesian Missionary Fellowship. While there he reported on the Muslim breakthrough in Serawai and requested the Institute to send an evangelist to the area. A student ready to do his practical work was assigned. Several weeks later the school's celebrated evangelist, Petrus Octavianus, led a team of students to the area. As a result of this tour, a large number of key persons in the Serawai tribe became firm believers in Christ. A church was formed which grew to three hundred members within a few months.

The new Christians almost immediately faced persecution for their faith. Other Islamic groups in the area tormented the converted Muslims through a malicious variety of harassments and threatened to put them to death if they would not recant. The central marketplace was divided into two areas—one for the "people" (the Muslims) and another for the Christian "dogs." Christians working with Muslims in the rice fields would not be given their fair share of the produce. When the new believers persisted in their faith despite the maltreatment, Muslims intensified their abuse. Burnings and beatings proved more persuasive. Two-thirds of the fledgling Christian population reverted to Islam, at least outwardly.

Then a seemingly fatal blow struck the depleted congregation—the severe illness of their pastor left them leaderless. But the congregation tenaciously carried on, supporting each other in the faith and taking on the care of their stricken pastor. The deserters, impressed by the loyalty of the persevering remnant and ashamed of their own defection, gradually returned. A year later, in the summer of 1965, the restored three hundred welcomed a second team of evangelists from Batu, three young missionaries who worked zealously with the local believers. The Christian group in the area soon tripled, and a Bible school was established in Tandjung Enim to train leaders to serve the new congregations.

That fall the Christian movement was again threatened when the nationwide Communist purge gave fanatical Muslims a chance to attack the Christians. It was easy to link many Christians with condemned Communists—some had once been actively associated with the Party. Others had unwittingly become attached to a Communist-front organization by their membership in a local farmers' union. And the fact that the Christians offered refuge to distraught Communists was clearly observable. But before the Sumatran Muslims could repeat the ravage of suspected Communists that occurred on Java, God intervened.

Shortly before the abortive coup a Sulawesi Christian had been appointed police inspector over the southern Sumatra area. To protect the threatened new believers from Muslims, he ordered all who were in danger of being purged placed in prison as "Communist sympathizers" along with the actual Communists who were being rounded up. In prison the Christians encouraged one another and boldly shared their faith with the Communists, who were so impressed by the believers' confident attitude that many were converted. What had begun as a plot to destroy Christianity actually served to spread it farther. When passions cooled and prisoners were released, a body of believers larger than the number originally jailed emerged

Pastor Dandra (left), leader of a widespread evangelistic work in southern Sumatra, visits a friend in Djakarta, H. F. Tan, pastor of a Chinese congregation.

to disperse the gospel throughout southern Sumatra.

The leader of this expanding Christian work in the south Sumatran jungles is a 36-year-old Sumbanese by the name of Dandra, who still encounters the fanaticism of Muslim zealots. I had met him in Djakarta, where he told me that a Christian school building in his area was recently burned and Christian homes were stoned by Muslim antagonists. The believers, however, had refused to be intimidated.

Not long before this, Dandra added, the leader of an area mosque had lost his hearing.

When he was visited by the local Christian pastor and an evangelist from Batu, the Muslim priest challenged the two: "If Christ is the Son of God, let him heal me." The evangelist placed his hands on the priest's ears and prayed for healing. When the "amen" was spoken, the Muslim heard wind blowing past his ear! He is now a staunch member of the local Christian fellowship.

Learning of this and other examples of Christian activity in Sumatra, I keenly anticipated my visit to the island's province of North Sumatra which encompasses Batakland, the original home of Frederick Tobing and the site of heralded mass conversions to Christianity. But I was to become a victim of my own overexpectation.

I felt initially a sense of disappointment at the conduct of some of the Sumatran Christians. A number whom I queried appeared to possess a shallow understanding of the faith. Their decision to become Christians often seemed more a hasty expedient than a lasting commitment. No doubt my weariness, not only from extensive travel in the equatorial heat but also from the news of my mother's death which I had received shortly before my Sumatra jaunt, affected my outlook.

I realized the extent of my fatigue during a question-and-answer session with a Karo Batak gathering one evening. My mind refused to phrase any further questions, and the interview would have been ruined had it not been for my quick-thinking host, Michael Dunn, a Britisher serving with the Overseas Missionary Fellowship. He produced a logical series of questions and then interpreted the Karos' answers for me.

The Reverend Mr. Dunn, assisted by his wife, Diana, a medical doctor, conducts a ministry in North Sumatra among great numbers of people stepping out of animism into Christianity. Observing his wide-ranging activity among these converts for whom Christianity represents a new way of life, I could appreciate his task.

I had learned about the training problems of the Batakland church in an earlier conversation in Djakarta. George Steed, Indonesian director of Overseas Missionary Fellowship, told me OMF began working among churches of the Karo tribes in 1961. The young missionary couple sent there set up a program of evangelism and lay training with a heavy emphasis on Bible teaching, and it bore quick fruit. By 1964 Karo Bataks rejecting animism were being baptized at the rate of 2,000 every year.

The OMF program profited from the government emphasis on education that had begun with independence in 1949. Educated Bataks could no longer support animistic beliefs, and were open to a new faith. Since pork has always been an important part of

Karo Batak women of North Sumatra sing in their dirt-floor chapel. OMF missionary Dr. Diana Dunn (extreme right) joins in.

the Batak diet, Christianity had that advantage over Islam, which forbids the eating of pig meat.

Karo church leaders realized the new converts would require thorough training in the faith, but before adequate arrangements could be made, the Communists grasped for power in Djakarta, causing even larger numbers to turn to Christianity in Batakland. With the government edict that every Indonesian claim allegiance to some religious faith, the Karo church saw a tenfold increase in the number of yearly baptisms. On Easter day in 1966, following the coup attempt of the previous September, more than 1,500 Karo tribespeople were baptized. The number of Karo Batak baptisms has averaged nearly 20,000 every year since.

"Unfortunately, the bigger the snowball got, the shallower was the teaching," Steed pointed out. "As things began to mushroom the next village down the way would call someone to teach them; and the church would send two or three workers in for long sessions, hour after hour, night after night. Then after a reasonable time they would have a baptism." The Karo membership doubled, then tripled, and today numbers close to 100,000. "These people desperately need Christian teaching," Steed acknowledges, "and that's what our missionaries are trying to do."

In the Medan area alone, where the Dunns are working with two Indonesian leaders, there are more than 10,000 relatively new converts to nurture. The statement of Christ that "the harvest truly is plenteous, but the laborers are few" holds singular meaning for the Karo workers. They don't take lightly his subsequent command to pray for harvest helpers.

Indonesia's compulsory education is playing an increasingly significant role in the spiritual development of the new Christians—not only in Batakland but throughout the country. A government ruling requires that some form of religion must be taught to all school children in addition to academic courses. If there are ten or more pupils requesting instruction in a specific religion, the government is committed to providing it. To help them carry out this ambitious promise, government educators asked the Indonesian Council of Churches, which adheres to an orthodox theology, to prepare a Christian curriculum. Having no course of study available at the time, the Council asked the OMF for help in drawing one up.

For the OMF it was a case of being in the right place at the right time with the right personnel. For years they had worked in mainland China as the China Inland Mission. When the Communists took over that giant country in 1949, the CIM was forced to relocate its many workers. Rechristened the Overseas Missionary Fellowship, the organization placed the China workers in various parts of East Asia, including Indonesia, which had just gained its independence and was welcoming Christian mission teams. Thus the OMF was on the scene when the Council of Churches made its request for help in building a curriculum. A qualified worker was assigned the task, and her Bible study books were accepted by the government for use in public schools. Many of the nation's 2,000 Christian schools use the books as well. In OMF Director Steed's words: "How more strategic can you get?"

Once again, the problem of providing the necessary manpower presents the biggest hurdle in carrying out the program's potential. In situations where no qualified teacher is available to teach the Bible course, Christian students must undergo instructions in an alien religion in order to meet graduation requirements.

I ran into a product of this unfortunate circumstance while touring ancient Buddhist and Hindu shrines in Jogjakarta. My tour guide was a vivacious young woman just out of college who illustrated a comment about the area's religious pluralism with a personal reference: "My father is Catholic; my mother is Christian [the general term for "Protestant" used by Indonesians]; and I am Muslim." "How do you happen to be Muslim with Christian parents?" I asked. "I learned it in school," she replied.

With its multiplying membership, the Karo Batak Church has been thankful for assistance from a variety of sources, including the helping hand of a neighbor. A sister fellowship, the Batak Protestant Christian Church which is composed largely of Toba tribespeople, has helped the Karos administer their large baptism rites in recent years. Much earlier the Tobas conducted their own mission work among the Karos. A keen interest in missions has, in fact, characterized the Toba church

117

during its hundred-year history—which may well explain why it is now the largest single church body in Indonesia, with nearly a million members.

The Toba church got its start in 1861, when Rhenish Missionary Society workers gained their first Christian converts in the area. In the latter part of the century the ever-growing church began dispatching its own evangelists to neighboring tribes, including the Karos. In 1930 the Toba Batak Church achieved autonomy, the first of Indonesia's churches to do so.

Unfortunately, schisms have marked the recent history of the church. While I was in Medan, I noticed two imposing buildings standing near each other and was told they represented rival Toba factions. Nevertheless, I was able to perceive the missionary spirit of the Toba church—which today holds membership in the Indonesia Council of Churches and the Lutheran World Federation. I talked with a local lay leader whose diligent work for his denomination's mission program had earned him a seat at the 1968 Asian Conference on Evangelism in Singapore. I was equally impressed by his description of his congregation's Medan Mission, an outreach to non-Christian Bataks.

This and other contacts I had with the variety of Christian activity on Sumatra pointed out for me the diversity of methods the Holy Spirit uses. Though the phenomena of the Timor revival and the power of the Batu evangelists are the most spectacular signs of revival in Indonesia, they are far from the only means God is employing. This fact was underscored for me while I was a guest of OMF missionaries Don Wylie, an Australian, and his American wife, Sybil.

They told me, for example, of a former Muslim who became a Christian through his diligent study of—not the Bible, but the Koran, the Islamic scriptures. Rifai Burhanu'ddin not only became a believer in Christ but has had a fruitful ministry pointing other Muslims to the Messiah. He is the author of *Jesus Christ and the Koran,* a definitive study of the Koran's references to Christ and an exposition of the Christian gospel, which has been instrumental in leading many Muslims to Christianity.

There is Stephanus, superintendent of a Sunday school established on a tobacco plantation by the Wylies. Early in his life Stephanus had made two major decisions: he rejected the Islamic faith of his parents; and, dissatisfied with being "nothing," he decided to investigate the Christian religion. He entered a small church in Djakarta one Sunday morning and first heard the gospel of Christ. In October 1957 at the age of nineteen Stephanus was baptized a Christian in the warm waters of the Java Sea. But he was not a happy Christian. The church he joined insisted that its members had to receive the gift of speaking in unknown tongues as a test of the indwelling of the Holy Spirit before salvation was accomplished. Stephanus had already experienced God's work within his life—subduing a quick temper and controlling worldly desires—and he waited expectantly for this power. But it didn't come. As months passed and Stephanus was unable to speak in tongues, his pastor insisted that he could not have salvation until he received this sign of the Holy Spirit.

In 1963 the young convert went to North Sumatra to become a plantation clerk. There he gave up his vigil and stopped going to church, convinced that for some reason he was ineligible for salvation. In his despondency, however, he picked up his Bible and opened it to the Gospels, where he happened to read Christ's promise of salvation and the Holy Spirit to all who would believe in him. Heartened by this revelation, Stephanus sought fellowship with biblical Christians and found it in a Javanese church that had been started in Medan. Later he met the Wylies and asked them to start a Sunday school for plantation workers. His deep Christian conviction can be readily seen, especially in the love he displays toward the Sunday school attendants and his own beautiful family.

There came also my own special experience of God's grace. Shortly before I left the islands, a feeling of depression came over me as I thought of leaving the tropical paradise and its friendly people. I wanted to return to my family, of course, but the realization that my mother would not be there to greet me blunted the prospect of that reunion. It had been nearly a week since I had received word of her death but, probably because of my fast-paced traveling, it wasn't until that afternoon that I felt so keenly the loss. Never again would I see her to joke with her and hear the many anecdotes she liked to recall.

Mustering the trust I had witnessed among the Indonesian Christians, I asked the Lord to help me through that hour. It was then that I was given the comforting assurance that my mother, who loved the Lord, was now with him and was enjoying the absolute bliss of heaven, no longer suffering from the painful agony of cancer. The sorrow I'd felt, I realized, was for myself. My grief was nothing more than self-pity. I asked God's forgiveness and my soul was flooded with his love. Just as the Bible promises, my sorrow was turned to joy. The assurance I received at that moment has never left me.

I accompanied Don Wylie to another unforgettable event. We took a long jaunt to a rubber plantation where he was to conduct a Sunday evening Bible study. Because of the

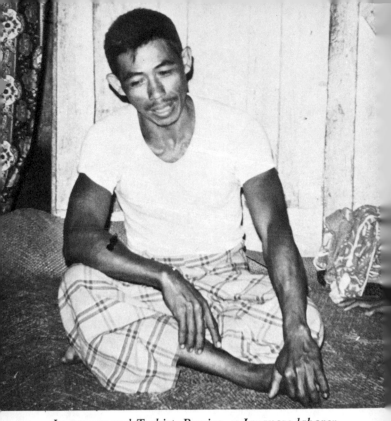

In sarong and T-shirt, Pawiro, a Javanese laborer in North Sumatran rubber plantation, sits on his home's only living room furniture, a coarse grass mat.

distance of the trip, Don planned an overnight stay. Our journey to the highlands took us through the hauntingly beautiful tropical forest country of North Sumatra. Occasionally from the road I could see the rubber trees slowly dripping snow-white latex from their slashed trunks into waiting buckets.

At dusk Don drove into a plantation drive and stopped near a long, one-story building. Standing in the doorway at the far end of the workers' apartments was a smiling Javanese gentleman in a T-shirt and sarong. Don introduced me to Pawiro, who invited us to step inside. Following Don's example, I removed my shoes in the small entryway and then entered the main room, where I met Pawiro's smiling wife and two grinning children. Aside from the grass mat that covered the floor, a few plastic flowers on a shelf, and a couple of framed prints of Jesus that were hanging on one of the rough board walls, the room was devoid of any furnishings. We were soon joined by four men, and the wife and children of one of the men. We squatted together on the floor mat for the Bible study.

After the study session, when I had an opportunity to talk to the small band, I discovered yet another way in which God had reached his Indonesian children. With this group it was a quiet working of the Spirit, albeit in a sometimes violent atmosphere. There were no manifestations of the miraculous other than that greatest of miracles, personal salvation. There was no large-scale turning to Christianity. In fact, the group had lost a number of members. But there was a resolute faith among the few believers that had survived the test of persecution.

Pawiro's journey into Christian faith began in his homeland of Java, in Jogjakarta, where he was earning a meager subsistance as a *betjak* driver. One Sunday a passenger in his pedicab, a Chinese gentleman whom he frequently cycled to church, handed him a Catholic catechism. Pawiro read the book with difficulty, since his formal education had been limited, but what he could understand from it about creation and salvation intrigued him. At least it provided more of a basis of faith than a sultan's proclamation that everyone in his jurisdiction was Muslim by official decree. Although Pawiro's identification papers listed him as Islamic, his family's faith was actually Buddhism. Pawiro's unprincipled life-style was not suddenly altered by his reading of the catechism, however. When he accepted an offer to go to North Sumatra as a plantation laborer early in 1968, he brought along the wife of another man. He also brought his Catholic catechism.

At the rubber plantation Pawiro met two other Javanese workers, Saidi and Hiro Karto, with whom he sensed a kinship. In their occasional evening get-togethers Pawiro learned that Saidi and Hiro Karto, like himself, felt detached from the Muslim religion they supposedly followed. He brought out his catechism and the three began to examine it. Their infrequent meetings became regular study periods as the Christian doctrine slowly unfolded for them. They sometimes discussed their evening studies on the job during the day. Then the plantation foreman, a zealous Muslim, called Pawiro into his office.

The foreman got right to the point. "I understand you've been holding some kind of religious meeting in your quarters. Since you're supposed to be a Muslim, why don't you go to the mosque?"

As best he could Pawiro explained the group's interest in Christianity that had been kindled by the catechism. "We are trying to understand it because we feel it speaks the truth. Don't we have that right?"

"Of course," the foreman admitted. "But I would like to see this catechism."

"We'll bring it to you tonight," Pawiro promised.

That evening he returned to the foreman's office with Saidi and Hiro Karto. The brief but significant session ended with the foreman retaining the catechism and the Javanese trio more determined than ever to study Christianity. The question of how to continue their study without the catechism was answered by a member of the plantation's security patrol. The policeman, a Toba Batak Christian, agreed to meet with the group to explain biblical doctrine.

Their training in Christianity was to continue—but so was the antagonism of the foreman. In September, through their patrolman friend, the group learned about an evangelistic meeting planned for a community nine miles away. The three families decided to attend and also to invite fellow workers. The latter decision, innocently conceived, would bring them some anxious moments.

Three days before the meeting, several Muslim laborers went around to the homes of the Javanese workers, loudly threatening to harm their families if they continued their apostasy. The following night the assistant foreman, also a Muslim, visited each home in the interest of fair play to encourage the Javanese *not* to be afraid of the intimidations. Despite the uncertainty of the outcome, Pawiro, Saidi, Hiro Karto, their families, and a few inquisitive workers attended the evangelistic meeting. It was at this meeting that Don Wylie first met the Javanese trio. It was at this meeting that eighteen new believers, including the plantation workers, stood to proclaim their acceptance of Christ.

The challenge of the Muslim mob, which did not immediately retaliate, appeared to be no more than an empty threat. A Christian congregation was formed at the plantation, an itinerant Indonesian preacher added the rubber farm to his circuit, and Don Wylie started his Bible class there. Things seemed to be going smoothly—until the congregation started to grow. Among the frequent visitors was the clerk of the plantation, a Karo Batak by the name of Nampaikan who was present at the Bible study the night of my visit. By the end of 1968 eleven families were counted in the congregation.

To celebrate their first Christmas season that year, the group planned a holiday program, with traditional carol singing and a uniquely Indonesian feature, an all-night puppet shadow play. The program drew the attention of the plantation workers, to the chagrin of the avid Muslims. They were quick to react. Whenever a member of the new Christian congregation would visit another citizen of the largely Islamic plantation community, Muslims would follow with a visit of their own asking questions about the previous conversation and making known the dire consequences of turning from Islam.

Dramatizing their seriousness, the Muslim zealots stormed Hiro Karto's home one night, wielding razor-sharp bark slashers as weapons. He managed to escape into the brush. Saidi was trapped in his home by angered Muslims, but he managed to talk them out of any violence. The harassment of the Muslims had its effect. Several families disassociated themselves from the Christians. Then plantation managers, seeking to restore calm to their community, dismissed the truculent foreman and the threats ceased.

The following June Hiro Karto, Pawiro,

and Saidi, with Nampaikan and other new believers, were baptized. It was not a frivolous ritual; they knew the gravity of such a step. Each had carefully considered the cost of following Christ. All had yielded to God's Spirit—and he had proven faithful to their trust.

When my interview ended and Pawiro's guests had gone, I followed Don into the small room where we were to sleep. Like the parlor, our bedroom held no furnishings other than the grass mat that covered the floor. Sleep did not come easily to me that night. It wasn't just the hardness of the ground that made me wakeful. The fact that I would be leaving Indonesia soon preyed on my mind. I couldn't help but compare my accommodations here with my surroundings in Djakarta when I had basked in a luxury hotel with its air-conditioning, comfortable beds, hot and cold running water, and flush toilets. But I would never exchange for those plush trappings the opportunity to be with the humble plantation believers who had found absolute contentment in knowing Jesus Christ.

9

Problems in Paradise

"Selamat Sore!" I bade a khaki-uniformed gentleman sitting in the foyer of the inn, smugly using the appropriate Indonesian greeting for that time of day.

"Good evening! How are you this evening?" the man replied in perfect English. I halted my stroll to an interview appointment and studied the speaker. He definitely was Indonesian in appearance, but his English was flawless.

"You speak very good English," I said.

"I learned it in Australia—in medical school," he told me. "What brings you to Indonesia?"

"I'm here on a writing assignment," I replied, "gathering information about the religious awakening here. Are you a doctor?"

"Yes, I'm a government medical inspector. I'm checking the hospital here."

"Oh, I've met the hospital director," I said with enthusiasm. "I understand he became a Christian during the revival here in Soé."

The doctor frowned. "Oh, yes?" he said slowly. "Could I ask you: how do you feel about the strange occurrences that have been reported here?"

"I find them extremely intriguing," I answered. "The people I've talked with are very sincere. Something out of the ordinary has certainly happened. Obviously, God has—"

"I just can't believe all the things that have been reported," the inspector interrupted. "Don't you find it a bit difficult to believe in water turning to wine and people being raised from the dead?"

"These things are foreign to me, too," I agreed, "but I'm certain that God has the ability to do such acts even though I've never personally experienced them. As a Christian, I believe that God has all power."

"I'm a Christian, too," the doctor emphasized, "but I'm not able to accept the idea that God works like that today." He concluded our conversation with a confidential smile and these disturbing words: "The Timorese have always been known as good storytellers."

This dialogue in Soé illustrates the troubling divergence of attitudes toward the Indonesian revival that I encountered during my stay. With the growth of Christianity on the islands so extraordinary that religious publications around the world have heralded it and even secular media such as the *Washington Post* and *Time* magazine along with the wire services have recorded it, one might assume that Indonesian Christians would be thoroughly and unanimously elated at being partner to such a singular blessing. Such is not the case.

Disagreement and dissension about the nature and extent of God's work divides the participants and observers of the movement. In many cases the dispute is tempered by love, but it nevertheless exists—and it is only one of many problems accompanying Indonesia's Christian awakening. I do not mean to disparage any of the people involved nor detract from God's obvious invasion of Indonesian life, but it would be dishonest to present the Christian expansion in these islands as being unhampered with troubles. Certainly here, as elsewhere that God has manifested his Spirit, Satan is waging a determined battle. Part of the miracle of Indonesia's spiritual renaissance is surely that it flourishes despite formidable obstacles.

Theological differences of opinion about the religious movement extend from open antagonism to unqualified acceptance. One missionary told me bluntly in reference to the reported miracles: "I believe the Timorese have an overactive imagination." Another was more charitable: "I like to keep an open mind, but I find it difficult to understand songs being taught by birds and stones." A mission official in Djakarta found it easy to accept reports of healings—"I've seen this myself as a field missionary"—but he questioned the reliability of the resurrection accounts and suggested that the emphasis upon the sensational aspect of the movement was misdirected. A missionary on the island of Timor, however, could find no reason to disbelieve or decry such miracles. "I have seen the 'impossible' happen here in the mountain areas even before the current revival," he told me. "The miracles have always been accompanied by a significant turning to the Christian faith by observers."

A degree of harmony has been maintained among a surprisingly wide range of biblical Christians in Indonesia, but strong unity is hampered by the divergent viewpoints of the various groups—which include Pentecostals, fundamentalists, evangelicals, and members of the Indonesia Council of Churches. Unfortunately, an air of suspicion taints relations between some of these groups, such as between members and nonmembers of the Council, though the Council supports an orthodox Christianity. Where the doctrinal gulf is broad, one might expect some friction. In certain areas, for example, Roman Catholic missions have been accused of taking undue advantage of the current religious surge, moving into unchurched regions already visited by Protestant evangelists and declaring as "Catholic" whole villages where headmen are ready to accept Christianity. Unhappily, discord is present in some cases within one fellowship.

Even in Timor. There the charismatic manifestations have been most pronounced —and seemingly most disputed. Churches once in denominational fellowship are now at odds, with some congregations keenly supporting, others strongly resisting, the revival movement. The reason for the resistance is sometimes difficult to determine, especially by those in the movement who revel in God's wonderful blessings. Opponents of the movement apparently see no evidence of the Holy Spirit's activity, rejecting the "miracles" as fabrications that just don't happen in this era.

In conversations with officials of the Council of Churches in Djakarta, I discovered an eagerness to mend fences and to follow the Spirit's leading in the evangelization of Indonesia. The evangelism secretary of the Council, D. S. Marantika, expressed a strong desire to cooperate with all scripturally orthodox groups in pursuing this task. He spontaneously lauded the work of the Indonesian Bible Institute at Batu, the school credited with launching the disputed revival in the now-divided Timorese church. Perhaps in God's time, as old wounds heal and the spirit of cooperation penetrates the divided factions, the breach will be spanned.

The interchurch struggle is not the only hindrance to the work of the Spirit among Indonesia's Christians. Well-intentioned Westerners have brought confusion and sometimes embarrassment or worse to the believers, descending upon the islands with their high-powered evangelism or their cameras and tape recorders. A long-time Indonesian missionary, bewailing the influx of foreign evangelists after reports of Indonesian church growth reached the West, told me that "commitments" made at mass rallies could often be attributed more to Asian hospitality than to a real understanding and acceptance of Christianity. He also charged that much indiscriminate reporting of spectacular events with only cursory investigation had raised questions about the reliability of the total movement. Indeed, the reports had caused misunderstanding and embarrassment to the extent that I found it difficult to gain information from some important spokesmen.

Such rash reporting can be very harmful indeed. Fanatic Islamic sects have, in fact, reacted violently to the effusive accounts of large numbers of Muslims turning to Christianity. They have burned churches, stoned the homes of Christians, and inflicted personal injury. At the height of the reprisal fifteen churches in Makassar were demolished on Reformation Day of 1967 by members of a Mohammedan youth organization. In Medan, North Sumatra, seventeen people were killed when Muslim teen-agers clashed with Christians. With such hatred toward Christianity displayed by zealous followers of Mohammed, converted Muslims do not take lightly their decision to forsake the Islamic faith. Freedom of religion is assured by law in Indonesia, and victims of religious persecution can appeal to authorities for protection, but social ostracism cannot be regulated.

Although free from fanaticism, Hinduism

has likewise proven an obstinate barrier to the spread of Christianity in Indonesia. This faith, which was transported to the islands from India in the second century, is concentrated in Bali, the exotic isle that has lured many a traveler to her arrestingly beautiful shores. The Balinese, of course, are known throughout the world for their precise ritual dances, legendary ceremonial dramas, intricately detailed paintings, and finely sculptured wood carvings—all of which reflect their religiously-entwined culture.

Under Dutch rule, Bali was closed to Christian evangelism until 1929, when a Chinese bookseller working with the Christian and Missionary Alliance was permitted to preach among the Chinese. A few years later, when a CMA missionary publicly baptized over a hundred Balinese converts, the resultant outcry against Christianity prompted the government to withdraw the mission's permission to work there. Evangelists from the East Java Church took up the challenge, and the Bali Protestant Christian Church was established in 1932. This body had grown to about 3,500 members by 1963, when the only other significant break occurred in Hinduism's grip on Bali.

That year the sacred volcanic Mount Agung erupted, killing 1,500 people. The Balinese were shaken spiritually as well as emotionally at this upheaval on the "isle of the gods," especially since their national shrine, the splendid Besakih Temple, was partially destroyed. As Christians ministered to the thousands made homeless, distributing relief supplies contributed by churches around the world, the Balinese were deeply stirred by the faith of people who could survive a natural disaster without a terrible fear or distrust of their God. Many sought out pastors or evangelists for instruction in the Christian faith. Then dispute arose among church leaders over whether to instruct the Hindu inquirers before baptizing them, or to baptize and then instruct, and much of the initial enthusiasm of the new converts waned. Nevertheless, the Christian churches on Bali may have doubled their membership in the two years following the holocaust.

Christian groups in Bali are not now enjoying the burgeoning church growth that other parts of Indonesia are witnessing. I learned firsthand one of the difficulties in reaching Balinese Hindus with the message of Christ on my second trip to Bali (this one made by air instead of by bus). Having been successful this time in reaching my Denpasar contact by telephone from the airport, I hailed a "Bali Art Tours" taxi to get to his place. It was operated by three young men who seemed anxious to explain Denpasar's points of interest. They eagerly answered my questions about the many statues of Hindu

gods that guarded homes and graced inter-
sections along the way. In such an atmosphere it seemed natural for my guides to
talk about religion, and I enjoyed listening to
their explanation of the government's *Pantja
Sila,* which guarantees Indonesia's freedom of
worship.

Pointing out that as a Muslim he got
along well with his Hindu colleagues, one of
the young men asserted, "In Indonesia we all
live peacefully together." I refrained from
mentioning the numerous incidents of persecution experienced by Indonesia's Christians
at the hands of Muslims.

When the Muslim and one of the Hindus
had finished explaining their beliefs, I
prepared to tell the glories of Christianity.
"Well, I'm a Christian," I began—and got no
further.

"I know your Christian beliefs," the Hindu
interrupted me. "You believe in a triune
God: a Creator, his Son, and his Spirit." He
went on to give a fairly accurate description
of the Trinity, although the concept of these
three being one all-powerful God had apparently escaped him. "We Hindus have a trinity, too," he added, "so we are very much like
you Christians."

I wondered, since he had already indicated
that the worship of Brahma, the Hindu su-
preme spirit, also allows the concomitant
worship of hundreds of gods, how he could

possibly compare it to the Christian Trinity. Listening to his clarification, I realized the difficulty of explaining the truth of Christianity to Hindus.

Hindus honor three personifications of Brahma—the creator, Brahma; the destroyer, Siva; and the preserver or renewer, Vishnu. Most Hindus consider Brahma relatively unimportant because he has finished his work of creating, so they worship either Siva or Vishnu. The more numerous followers of Siva believe that by destroying, this god makes room for the new. The followers of Vishnu think of him as a god of love. They believe he has come to earth a number of times in different forms, and they worship these incarnations.

Before I could come up with a Christian apologetic to answer the guide, we had arrived at my destination. It was the home of CMA missionary Kenneth Van Kurin, who had started his work in Denpasar in 1962. Thanks to the *Pantja Sila,* the Alliance had been able to return to Bali after Indonesia gained independence. I introduced myself to my host and, as the cab drove away, commented about how frustrating it must be to work among Hindus if they were all like the young tour guide. Van Kurin assured me that this pluralistic attitude is indeed a stumbling block to his witness. But cultural barriers are even harder to surmount, he pointed out.

To illustrate, he cited his own experience in Bali.

A year after he had started his ministry in Denpasar, Van Kurin's congregation numbered about forty, but none of these were converts from Hinduism. Eight years later the congregation had grown to only sixty baptized members, two-thirds of whom came from Muslim rather than Hindu backgrounds. A score of Balinese, also attending regularly, had professed belief in Christ but had not made the final break with Hinduism that baptism signified. Almost all of the few former Hindus who had been baptized had been separated from their Balinese culture before leaving Hinduism. Some, for example, were servants working in the homes of Christians. Others had married Christian spouses.

Why are the Balinese so reluctant to renounce Hinduism? A major reason is that in doing so one must relinquish his very way of life. Almost every function in the Balinese Hindu's routine of daily living is performed ritually, from his medicine-man-attended birth to his elaborate ceremonial cremation. The work in the field, the preparation of food, the frequent offerings to household gods are all dictated by the law of *Karma,* which teaches that a person's deeds in this life determine the next life he'll lead—in a series of reincarnations aimed at ultimate union with Brahma.

Social strictures keep the Hindu believer in line. If he leaves his home to settle in a new community, he will likely be asked upon arrival, "Where are you from?" followed by "Why did you leave?" If the person reveals that he has become a Christian, he may well be told, "The road out of the city is this one, and you may take it."

Van Kurin sees few ways to break the social fetters that bind the Balinese Hindus. A promising proposal is to reach the many young people who come to Denpasar to find employment. A planned youth center there would provide a means for young villagers arriving in the city to escape their structured cultural backgrounds. In such a setting Christianity could be clearly and openly presented. Once grounded in Christianity, converts could take the gospel back to their own clan. Historically, indigenous evangelism has proven the most effective mission outreach. Hopefully, this long-range plan will eventually overcome the ethnic barriers that have long impeded Christian witness on this fallen paradise isle.

Cultural barriers of quite a different nature hamper the evangelization of Kalimantan, Indonesia's largest geographic segment. Occupying most of Borneo, the world's third-largest island, Kalimantan is a restless but still quiet giant. Its economic development has been slow, due to dense jungles harboring sometimes hostile headhunters, large coastal swamps, and towering inland mountains. Modern technology promises to facilitate the exploitation of Kalimantan's natural resources, but primitive transportation methods still frustrate Christian evangelism, which was permitted on a wide scale only after Indonesia's independence was gained in 1949.

Kalimantan's highways are her capricious rivers—when they are navigable. Shallow draft steamers are usually able to transport cargo a few hundred miles inland, after which river launches or smaller vessels must be used to navigate the tributaries. Travel in the interior is conducted largely on foot, sometimes with the aid of water buffalo.

A British missionary to Kalimantan told me that rivers played such an important role in his ministry, especially the visitation of outlying areas, that he scheduled his trips according to the level of the rivers. But he relied on God to insure their navigability. "The Lord provided so well for me that the tribespeople would plan their trips to coincide with mine," he remarked.

The limited accessibility of the region is reflected in the religious and cultural remoteness of Kalimantan's interior tribes, once known as the "wild men of Borneo." More properly called Dyaks, the tribes have largely relinquished their practice of decapitation, although in late 1967 they engaged in a vicious massacre and pillage of Chinese settlers to avenge the execution of a dozen of their people by Communist guerrillas.

While the Communist outlaws who fled to the Kalimantan jungles from other parts of Indonesia after the abortive coup continue to stir up trouble, the Dyaks are victims of a far more sinister enemy.

A host of spirits, which the Dyaks believe inhabit almost everything, keep the people shackled to rigid practices and precautions to ward off potential calamity. In their communal long houses, which range from thirty to a thousand feet in length according to the number of occupant families, amulets protect their rooms, beds, doors, cooking area, entryway, and, outside, their fields. "Every part of their lives is wrapped up in their worship of these fetishes," an American missionary told me.

So as not to offend the spirits who inhabit the amulets, tabus are established by each commune. Before entering a long house, a visitor must first rid himself of anything in his possession that violates a local code. Omens, such as the call of a certain bird, are also assiduously respected to the point of a Dyak's canceling an important trip or taking a more circuitous route to avoid the warned-of adversity. Within such an occult arena, witch doctors enjoy a thriving business, manipulating spirits through their sorcery to obtain a special advantage for a paying customer—or themselves—and further binding the people to the demons' sway.

"I've seen witch doctors perform unbelievable feats of magic—even to willing a person's death," the American declared. "They obviously are in league with demonic spirits. And anyone who has worked in this area knows there are such things as evil spirits." To illustrate the reality of the demonic power, he told of a visit he had made with a national evangelist to one long house.

The villagers, who had briefly heard an evangelist earlier and were eager to learn more about Jesus, welcomed the couple cordially and assured them they need not fear for their safety. "But," the two were warned, "don't go near the spirit tree." The fearsome tree was pointed out to the visitors as its awesome history was recounted. As long as the villagers honored the tree, keeping a respectful distance and worshiping the spirit within it, their crops prospered. On different occasions, however, three skeptical youths had foolishly tested the power of the tree. All had died within twenty-four hours after touching its bark. To the surprise of all the villagers as well as my informant, the evangelist asked for an axe and proceeded to chop the spirit tree down. Wails of doom did not deter him. When the tree was finally felled, the evangelist set it afire.

"You are a foolish man," a village elder told him. "You will not live through the night."

"We'll see," was his reply.

The following day the evangelist, alive and well to the surprise of all the villagers, did not deny the might of the tree's spirit. "It had lots of power," he told his astonished listeners, "but Jesus Christ has more." The incident convinced many of the villagers and marked the start of a Christian congregation.

Victories like this, however, must be repeated many times to make inroads in spiritism's control of such areas as the interior of Kalimantan. A similar situation exists in West Irian, Indonesia's half of New Guinea, the world's second-largest island. As in Kalimantan, the marshy coastal plains, high mountain ranges, tropical jungles, and traditionally antagonistic tribes of West Irian have proven massive obstacles to a widespread Christian awakening.

Of the numerous and varied spiritual battles being fought in Indonesia today, however, the fiercest and most significant are undoubtedly those being waged by individuals. Temptation seems to be heaped upon the person who would serve Christ to the utmost. As in other contests threatening God's work throughout the islands, the Enemy sometimes wins. In more than one interview I was told of once-zealous Christians who had "fallen into sin" and lost their spiritual gifts. Some had become inordinately proud of their presence at a supernatural event or perhaps at their ability to call down divine healing. Others became victims of what one knowledgeable observer described as a "woeful" moral climate. "Premarital sex experience, particularly among teen-agers, is an institutionalized normality here," he declared. Fine youths who had seemed destined for promising ministries have sacrificed their unique spiritual blessing for this temporal pleasure.

But the failure of some has been a lesson for others. Those who recognize the viciousness of the temptations they confront and rely wholly on God for power to resist them form the strong core of Indonesia's revival leadership. No doubt the uncommon faith of these humble Christians, who trust implicitly in God's ability to accomplish mighty deeds, accounts for the incredible works performed in Indonesia.

Why then should a reporter spend so much time on the spiritual problems when there is so much to praise God for? To induce the concerned reader to pray—effectively—for God's faithful Indonesian servants who battle many foes.

10

Tomorrow . . .

"But will it continue?"

I've heard this question asked of the Indonesian spiritual movement by a surprising variety of people—by those intimately involved in it and by those candidly opposed to it; by those who witness it in person and by those who view it from a distance. To casual observers it may seem merely an academic query, but it is an essential question to those who are deeply concerned that there are many islanders who have yet to hear about God's Son. Will this season of the Spirit's visit fade, they wonder, from ineffective utilization of such great power? Or will it continue until all have been told? While God alone will ultimately reveal the answer, the history of the revival since its major impetus was felt in 1965 affords a number of clues about its life expectancy.

In assessing the unusual spiritual activity in Indonesia, most church leaders would agree with the missionary who told me, "The revival has matured; it's lost the flamboyance that characterized its early stages when every miracle story got juicier with the telling, and the people were flocking to the churches to save their hides." These leaders expect God to continue to bless their efforts to spread the gospel, although they believe the dramatic manifestations of the Spirit may decline.

"I think the Church in Indonesia is going to keep right on growing," declared Frank L. Cooley, an American Presbyterian missionary who is conducting a broad analytical study of the country's Christian movement for the Indonesia Council of Churches. "I see the Holy Spirit very active on a wide variety of fronts, in some places where we don't even look for it," he told me. The massive movement to Christianity has created healthy problems for the churches, he believes. "They're struggling with their statements of faith and seeking ways to make the gospel more relevant. The ecclesiastical position has been subjected to biblical analysis, and some inherited positions have been altered with biblical insight. This is evidence to me of the depth of the Holy Spirit's work here."

I was struck by the confident reply of Sardjito Martosudarmo, principal of the Bible school in Soé, Timor, when I asked if he felt the Holy Spirit was just as active now as earlier in the revival. "Oh, yes!" he exclaimed and then related what had happened just the day before my arrival in Soé.

A friend of Sardjito's, a member of one of the evangelistic teams, was visiting a patient in the government hospital in Soé. While standing at the bedside, the man received a vision from the Lord that the patient was hiding certain fetishes—a root of a plant, a cord, and some daggers. He told the sick man what God had revealed to him and admonished: "You must surrender them so you can be well again." Overwhelmed by this revelation, the patient admitted his guilt and told where the fetishes could be found. The team member collected the *djimats* and took them to Sardjito. After praying for God's protection over the team and the man who had surrendered the fetishes, Sardjito burned the root and cord and destroyed the daggers. He then went to pray with the patient, who soon recovered.

The attitude of Sardjito and other national Christians like him is: "Why shouldn't God keep on blessing in this way if we are subject to his will?"

In a sense the spiritual movement in Indonesia is self-perpetuating. All of the mission or indigenous groups I encountered had drafted plans to expand their current involvement. The Christian and Missionary Alliance, for example, anticipates an extension education program to give requested evangelism training to Indonesian pastors and laymen. As this is written the Missionary Aviation Fellowship is opening up new possibilities by enabling organizations to enter areas heretofore virtually inaccessible. Among indigenous groups, particularly, there is a compelling urgency to evangelize because "Jesus is coming soon."

I could feel this budding evangelistic spirit as I sat at the Scheunemann dinner table at the Bible school in Batu, East Java. Dining with me one evening were a young lady who had just returned from Djakarta, having spent her year of practical training there bringing the love and knowledge of Christ to prostitutes; two women graduates who had taken the Christian message into Portuguese Timor, that half of the island still under colonial rule—nominally Catholic but largely animistic; and an Indonesian instructor at the school who had traveled with a team to Pakistan to conduct a fruitful campaign against the dangers of witchcraft.

Evidence of an accelerating movement to Christianity is now emerging from previously unresponsive parts of Indonesia. In the spring of 1971 the Worldwide Evangelization

Crusade field leader in Kalimantan, Fred Woodward, filed an enthusiastic report about an unusual response by that island's isolated Dyaks:

"In the Upper Kapuas region new tribes are responding in areas we had not yet evangelized. Among one tribe with whom we have labored for many years great numbers are now turning to the Lord. Invited by the Christian and Missionary Alliance, WEC workers moved up the mighty Kapuas River beyond all existing missionary outreach in 1949. Our goal was to bring the gospel to twenty unevangelized Dyak tribes. After twenty years of laborious effort by a handful of workers, only ten tribes had some who were born again. But in the last two years the change has been tremendous. The number of both workers and Christians has doubled. When I prepared the annual report for the department of religion two months ago, there were 3,300 professing Christians! And things are moving so rapidly these days that probably 500 have been added to that number since!"

Later that summer students from the Batu Bible institute entered Ketapang, a remote region of Kalimantan isolated by natural barriers, for the first Christian witness there. "After only two months of ministry, seventeen villages responded to the gospel," a spokesman reported. "The young people continued trekking on foot from village to village, often as far as twenty miles. After six months approximately 3,000 believed on Jesus Christ. Converts include witch doctors who have burned their amulets and charms."

Earlier a Timorese evangelist, working with his wife in West Irian, witnessed victory in an area where Western missionaries had labored forty years among people clinging to witchcraft. In December, 1970, Franz Selen brought six tribes together for a ceremonial burning of fetishes and a mutual profession of faith in Christ.

Another Timorese, Mel Tari, felt led by God to make an evangelistic tour in 1971 throughout a country he had believed was a completely Christian nation until he arrived—the United States of America.

Surprisingly, there are some who refuse to believe that the Holy Spirit is doing anything unusual in Indonesia. These people do not deny that the churches have enjoyed increased membership since 1965—a gain of more than two million according to one estimate. But they maintain that the sudden interest in Christianity can be explained by factors other than a spiritual awakening: as a dodge to avoid being labeled Communist in the tumultous days following the abortive coup or in conformity to a government decree that every citizen claim a religion. With regard to the workings of the Spirit, they insist that the charismatic manifestations, if factual, have been overemphasized—to the detriment of the church as a whole. While there is a difference of opinion about the validity of the miracles within the revival movement, there is general agreement among Western observers that any religious experience by Indonesia's people would involve a confrontation with the occult. As one missionary put it: "It's only logical that God would work with mystical people in a mystical way."

It is a puzzling anomaly that some people who claim allegiance to the canon of Holy Writ, filled as it is with accounts of the miraculous, are so certain that a present-day performance of wonders by the Author of the Scriptures is impossible. The Indonesian revival has been accompanied by unique spiritual demonstrations—many truly mystifying. But who can explain the Bible accounts of these phenomena? Skepticism mounts highest, it seems, over the raising of the dead, as if this were too difficult or too sacred an act to entrust to human agents. Certainly, the familiar biblical resurrections of Lazarus, the Nain widow's son, and of course the Savior were effected directly by the Godhead. But fallible men have been permitted this privilege as well—notably Elijah, who raised a widow's son (1 Kings 17:17-24); and Peter, who prayed Dorcas back to life (Acts 9:36-41).

Even as I write these words, I realize that mere argument will fail to convince many. Acceptance of any miracle is a matter of faith. I can only attest that the witnesses from whom I received the reports were guilelessly serious and obviously Christ-ones.

At any rate, the dramatic spiritual convulsion that shakes Indonesia, however it is regarded, cannot be denied. And what is happening there may be the ground swell of a worldwide awakening. Reports of increasing Christian activity are coming out of Russia and other Iron Curtain countries. After more than twenty years of defiance, the most blatantly atheistic country in the world, China, opened her doors to the West in 1971, offering a sliver of new hope to the oppressed "silent" Christians of that vast land. Evangelism-in-depth programs of the Latin America Mission represent one of many effective means that have been successful during the past decade in reaching Central and South Americans with the Christian message. Adaptations of the LAM concept have been effectively used in the United States and Europe, considered to be the most difficult of mission areas today.

But there is much clearer evidence.

An article in a 1971 issue of *Christian Life* magazine reported an African revival that parallels Indonesia's: "From Sierra Leone in the West across the waistline of Africa to Tanzania, churches are doubling and tripling in membership. Some congregations have grown by 5,000 members in three years. . . . Plainly, it is the youth who are responding to the gospel, rejecting both the ancient animistic religions of their tribes and the harsh militancy of Islam. Yet so irresistible is the gospel to Africans that older people are also being converted."

And revival is coming to America, evangelist Billy Graham told the National Association of Evangelicals in the spring of 1971. A few weeks later his brother-in-law and associate evangelist, Leighton Ford, enumerated for members of the Evangelical Press Association seven signs of it: "A new interest in Christ in the news media; a resurgence of student power for Christ; new openness to the personal gospel among Roman Catholics; searching and spiritual wistfulness among adults; revived interest in the supernatural; a departure from old pietistic-activistic hang-ups; and renewed concern for evangelical action."

Time magazine, in its June 21, 1971, issue, carried a lengthy cover story of "The Jesus Revolution." Numerous other secular magazines and newspapers have likewise recognized the movement with a flood of features on the "Jesus People." As in Indonesia, divine healing, deliverance from demon possession, and other supernatural activity have been reported in the current spiritual movement in America.

The spiritual fire kindled in Indonesia and elsewhere around the world burns ever brighter as it finds new fuel among those yet to be reached. Its flame may well spread until that glorious day foretold by Christ when the gospel "shall be preached in all the world for a witness unto all nations."

The revival *will* go on. Will it go on through you?

And many other signs truly did Jesus in the presence of his disciples, which are not written in this book: but these are written, that ye might believe that Jesus is the Christ, the Son of God; and that believing ye might have life through his name.

—John 20:30, 31

INDEX-GLOSSARY